Get the most from this book

This book will help you revise the contents of OCR Cambridge Nationals in ICT Level 1/2 Unit 1. You can use the contents list on pages 4 and 5 to plan your revision, topic by topic. Tick each box when you have:

1 revised and understood a topic

2 tested yourself

3 checked your answers online

You can also keep track of your revision by ticking off each topic heading through the book. You may find it helpful to add your own notes as you work through each topic.

Tick to track your progress

Exam tip

Throughout the book there are Exam tips that explain how you can boost your final grade.

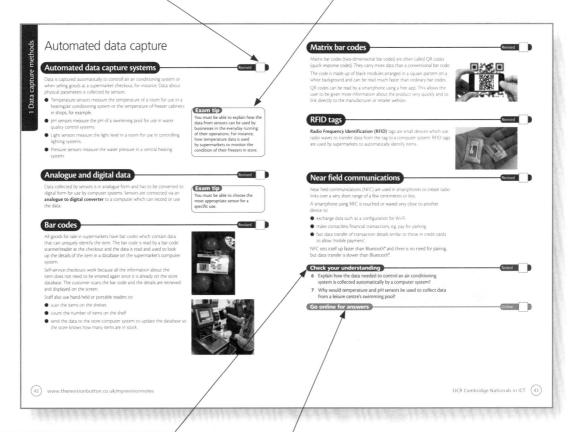

Check your understanding

Use these questions at the end of each section to make sure that you have understood every topic.

Go online for answers

Go online to check your answers at **www.therevisionbutton.co.uk/myrevisionnotes**

Contents and revision planner

LO1 — Understand how ICT can be used to meet business needs

LO2 — Know how to work with information and data to meet specified business needs

LO3 — Know how ICT can be used to support business working practices

LO4 — Understand how legal, ethical, safety and security issues affect how computers should be used

How ICT is used

Businesses, organisations and individuals use Information Technology in many ways.

How schools use ICT

Revised

Schools, colleges and universities use ICT for:

- advertising their courses and staff vacancies
- providing access to information about themselves as well for teaching and learning
- collecting data for tracking the performance of students and teachers
- administration tasks, such as writing letters and reports to parents
- supporting the teaching of students
- helping students learn by using computers in classes.

How businesses use ICT

Revised

Businesses and organisations such as estate agents or leisure centres use ICT for:

- selling services to customers
- planning and monitoring finances
- communications between staff
- communicating with customers.

An example – estate agent

Estate agent employees could use ICT in their offices to store details of properties and clients and when they are out and about, such as when showing prospective buyers around houses for sale or rent. Other examples of the use of ICT and computer devices by the staff at estate agents could include:

- using word processors and desktop publishing software to write advertising reports for a new house for sale
- using digital cameras (or the cameras in smartphones) to take digital images of houses for sale or rent
- using digital cameras (or the cameras in smartphones) to take digital images of the contents of houses for rent to make a record of the condition of the property and contents
- finding the location of and directions to houses for sale or rent using navigation software or global positioning systems (GPS) in smartphones or by using laptops and the internet
- using dedicated satellite navigation systems with GPS to navigate to and from houses for sale or rent.

Government services

Citizens can access information about government services via the internet to:

- complete and file tax forms online and make tax payments
- complete and confirm entries in an electoral register so they can vote
- apply for official documents, e.g. driving licences, passports, identification documents
- sign online petitions and questionnaires
- lobby politicians.

Governments use ICT to make information publicly available via websites and emails as well for creating and publishing documents.

Central and local government employees use ICT in their offices and when out on the government's business.

> **Exam tip**
>
> Look at the Health and Safety website: www.hse.gov.uk/legislation
>
> Look to see what documents are available and how the site links to social networking to give out information.
>
> Make sure that you know how government websites can be used to provide information and to apply for official documents.

Using ICT to shop online

Customers can use ICT to:

- research companies that they might wish to buy items from
- contact the companies, place and pay for orders
- track orders
- provide feedback to the company about what they think of their products and service.

Remote working

People can use ICT to work while away from the office, at home or travelling. They can:

- send emails to colleagues and customers
- access and transfer files on company servers or on cloud storage.

The system that stores the files for remote access must be:

- configured to allow remote access
- set up so the worker has the proper authentication to be allowed access
- able to send and receive files securely.

Remote access can involve:

- sharing the desktop of a computer in the office
- using a virtual private network (VPN)
- accessing files and folders using specialist software such as FTP.

The worker must have a user name and a password in order to access files.

Check your understanding

1 Make a list of the jobs that a receptionist at a medical centre would have to do and how ICT would be used in the job.

2 How would an estate agent representative use ICT when visiting a house that is about to go up for lease?

Go online for answers

The difference between desktop and portable systems

Desktop systems

Desktop computer systems are used in workplaces where employees need to access and use information, such as:

- offices
- shops
- warehouses
- libraries
- health and leisure centres.

Portable systems

Workers do not always need to be physically present in a workplace, instead they can work remotely, such as when working from home or travelling. Workers can access the same information as in their workplace using modern mobile communications systems.

Portable computers include:

- laptops
- netbooks
- tablet computers
- smartphones.

Portable computers can do most of the tasks required in business and are often used instead of desktop computers.

> **Exam tip**
>
> Make sure you know how desktop computers are different from portable systems like laptops and that you can match the features of each to their uses in businesses as well as in the home.

Check your understanding **Tested**

3 Why are desktop computers more suitable than laptops for employees that always work in offices?

Go online for answers **Online**

Portable computer systems

Laptops
Revised ☐

Laptops are portable because:

- they are lighter than desktop computers
- they can be powered by batteries
- the keyboard and pointing device are built in instead of separate
- the monitor is built in
- optical storage devices are usually built in
- connection to a network and/or the internet is usually wireless.

Laptops allow the user to be mobile but are easily damaged while being moved and are easy to steal.

Typical uses of laptops by businesses include:

- office-based tasks such as word processing and dealing with emails while away from the office and when travelling
- creating documents
- editing video or audio
- ● creating presentations
- instant messaging between employees and/or customers
- live web chat between employees and/or customers.

Netbooks
Revised ☐

Netbooks are:

- smaller and lighter than laptops
- easier to carry or use while travelling on trains and aircraft.

Netbooks are portable because:

- they are lighter than laptops or desktop computers
- they can be powered by batteries
- the keyboard and pointing device are built in instead of separate
- the monitor is built in
- storage of data can be on a solid-state disk or a magnetic hard disk, although they do not usually have built-in optical storage devices
- they use wireless connections to a network and/or the internet.

Netbooks allow the user to be mobile but, like laptops, are easily damaged while being moved and are easy to steal. They usually have a low specification so software applications that need fast processors and a lot of memory run slower or maybe not at all.

Typical uses of netbooks by businesses include office-based tasks similar to those performed on desktop and laptop computers, but the lower specification of netbooks means that tasks take longer and some cannot be done at all.

While out of the office, netbooks are most useful for:

- sending and receiving emails
- instant messaging
- live web chat
- browsing the internet.

Tablet computers

Tablets have a touch screen that can:

- display an on-screen keyboard for typing
- allow selection to be done with the fingers on screen
- respond to touch gestures such as swiping or pinching
- run an application that will take over the whole screen and hide other applications.

Tablet computers are portable because they:

- are usually smaller even than laptops or netbooks
- are lighter than laptops or desktop computers
- can be powered by batteries
- have no physical keyboard or pointing device
- often have a solid-state disk, or other flash memory, for storage of data.

Most office tasks can be done on tablet computers but users can find this awkward or difficult as the software may work in different ways than on desktops or laptops.

While out of the office, tablet computers are most useful for:

- sending and receiving emails
- instant messaging
- live web chat
- browsing the internet
- viewing photographs or images.

Smartphones

A smartphone is a mobile computer system that combines:

- mobile telephone
- personal digital assistant (PDA)
- web browser
- media player
- connections to the mobile phone network and to the internet via the phone network or a wireless network

- digital camera
- GPS system
- touch screen for input and output
- the ability to run applications (apps).

Smartphones are powered by batteries.

Business-related software applications (apps) are available that allow office tasks, and data exchange with company servers, to be carried out on smartphones.

Typical uses of smartphones by businesses include:

- telephone conversations with friends and colleagues
- keeping personal and business diaries
- using software applications (apps)
- sending and receiving mail
- sending and receiving text messages
- web browsing.

Exam tip

Make sure that you know how different people would use a smartphone and why a smartphone might be more useful to them than other portable computer systems.

Check your understanding
Tested

4 What features of a laptop enable it to be used away from an office environment?

5 Why are office tasks more difficult to carry out on netbooks than on laptops?

6 Why would a tennis coach working at a leisure centre prefer to use a tablet computer than a desktop computer?

Go online for answers
Online

Advantages and disadvantages of different types of computer system

Comparing desktop and portable systems

Revised

Type of computer system	Advantages	Disadvantages
Desktop computer	• High performance, can carry out all office tasks. • Replacing or upgrading components is easy. • Screen size can be very large. • Monitor and keyboard positioning can be adjusted.	• Fixed in one location. • Can be bulky.
Laptop computer	• Small and light so portable. • Built-in pointing device, keyboard and monitor. • Uses battery power.	• Damaged more easily. • Repairs and upgrades more difficult. • Battery life can be limited. • Easily lost or stolen. • Data can be less secure.
Netbook computer	• Very small and light so more portable. • Built-in pointing device, keyboard and monitor. • Longer battery power life.	• Lower specification than other computer types. • Damaged more easily. • Repairs and upgrades more difficult. • Do not have optical drives. • Easily lost or stolen. • Data can be less secure.
Tablet computer	• Very light and thin so highly portable. • Supports a variety of apps.	• Office tasks not easy to carry out using touch screen technology. • Limited connectivity to external devices. • Data can be less secure.
Smartphone	• Small and light so very portable. • Ideal for mobile communication, used for entertainment and web browsing.	• Office tasks difficult as device is too small. • Easily lost or stolen. • More care needs to be taken to keep data secure and safe.

Exam tip

You should make sure that you are familiar with the latest specifications for the different types of computer systems, their operating systems and how they differ, and their relative costs. This will be useful for deciding which computer system is best for a particular job or task or for use by different people such as receptionists, travelling salespeople or trainers at a leisure centre.

Check your understanding

Tested

7 Why do laptops and netbooks often have a lower specification than desktop computers?

8 Why are laptops and netbooks more difficult to upgrade and repair than desktop computers?

9 Why would a supermarket manager prefer to use a tablet computer and smartphone rather than a desktop computer?

Go online for answers

Online

Input devices

Keyboard
Revised ☐

A keyboard has keys that are labelled with characters set out in a pattern. It is used to enter characters such as letters, punctuation marks, numbers, and symbols. It can be used to enter commands into a computer or for typing letters, memos, reports or entering data into spreadsheets or databases.

Specialist keyboards
Revised ☐

Specialist keyboards have keys labelled with characters set out in a different pattern from an ordinary keyboard or with the raised marks of Braille to enter characters.

Specialist keyboards can be:

● designed for disabled users, e.g. Braille keyboards for the visually impaired

● engineering keyboards for specialised character entry.

Mouse
Revised ☐

A mouse is used to move a pointer on screen and has one or more buttons that are clicked to choose items from an on-screen menu and select items by clicking.

Microphone
Revised ✓

Microphones convert sounds to electrical signals which can be digitised. They are used when talking on a mobile phone or when using videoconferencing or audio chat.

Key pad
Revised ☐

A key pad has fewer keys than an ordinary keyboard: often only numbers and characters such as * and #. It can be used when entering the price or cost of an item.

Touch pad

Revised

A touchpad is a touch-sensitive panel that responds to fingers. It can be used instead of a mouse to move a pointer on screen or by tapping, which can act as a mouse click does.

Remote control

Revised

Remote controls input commands or instructions into computer systems or equipment and can be wired or wireless sending command signals to devices such as TVs or wheelchairs. In business they are used to control training equipment and TV displays.

Scanner

Revised

Scanners use reflected light from documents or photographs to capture a digital version of a document or image which can then be used in software applications such as word processors.

Bar code reader or scanner

Revised

These scan the lines or matrix of a bar code and convert them for input into a computer system. The captured bar code can be used to look up the details of an item in a database.

Chip and PIN reader

Revised

The chip in the card is read in a slot and there is a key pad for entering the PIN. A magnetic stripe reader is used if the chip cannot be read (or if a card has no chip). Card details are read from the card and checked using the PIN entered by the purchaser when using a credit or debit card.

Magnetic stripe reader

Revised

Reads the data from a magnetic stripe on the card when a card is 'swiped' through a slot in the reader. Data is read from the magnetic stripe if the card has no chip or the chip cannot be read when a credit or debit card is used.

MIDI

Revised

MIDI is a special interface for connecting musical instruments to computer systems and for storing and transmitting music data.

Sensors

Revised

Sensors convert physical variables, such as temperature, pressure or light, into electrical signals. They can be used for measuring the temperature or light levels of offices, which could then be used in controlling an air conditioning system.

Camera

Revised

Cameras use light sensitive receptors to convert light into electrical signals that are digitised and stored as still or moving images. They are used for taking photographs, capturing video or for video surveillance in CCTV.

Exam tip

You should make sure that you know the features and purpose of each input device and how it could be used in businesses. This will help you to decide on the most appropriate method of data entry in specific businesses.

Check your understanding

Tested

10 Why are specialist keyboards needed?

11 Describe two situations where a key pad would be more suitable than a full-size keyboard.

12 Why do laptops have touchpads?

13 Remote controls are common in the home. Describe how remote controls could be used in:

   a) a supermarket

   b) an estate agent office and

   c) by a trainer who coaches swimming.

14 Why do Chip and PIN readers also have magnetic stripe readers?

Go online for answers

Online

Output devices

Monitor
Revised

Monitors display the results of computer processing to the user. They can display characters as they are typed, video as it is played or can be used for watching CCTV images.

Printer
Revised

Printers produce hard copies of the results of processing. They could be used for printing membership cards, passes or receipts.

Laser printers can print large quantities of high quality copies in a short time and can have lower running costs in offices. Inkjet printers can produce high quality colour prints but are usually slower to print with higher running costs.

Plotter
Revised

Plotters are designed to print drawings onto large sheets of paper. They are used for printing designs and plans by businesses such as architects.

Actuators
Revised

Actuators are types of motors for controlling systems or mechanisms. A motor could be used to open an automatic door, move a conveyor belt at a supermarket checkout or turn on a water sprinkler by opening a valve.

Speakers, earphones, and headphones

Revised

These produce sounds for people to hear. They allow users to hear audio files, music, movie soundtracks and the voices of other people. They are used in smartphones and in audio or videoconferences.

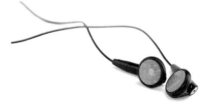

Data or digital projector

Revised

These project an enlarged image of a computer display onto a screen. They can be used for showing presentations to large numbers of people, such as members of staff.

Exam tip

For each of the devices shown, you must make sure that you know what they are used for and which is the most appropriate for specific tasks, e.g. printing large quantities of letters, printing very large diagrams in an architect's office or making posters for wall display.

Check your understanding

Tested

15 What type of printer would be the best choice for use by a receptionist for printing A4 posters to display on the wall, and why?

16 How would a salesperson trying to persuade a supermarket manager to sell his new range of fizzy drinks make use of a data projector?

Go online for answers

Online

Other devices

Touch screen

Revised

A touch screen is an input and an output device, so it has a dual function. It has the same purpose as any other monitor, but can also be used to input data. A user of a smartphone will use a touch screen.

Storage devices

Hard disk drive (HDD) using magnetic disks

Hard disk drives use magnetic disks for storing software and data in files. The disks are circular and spin at high speeds while drive heads read and write the data which makes hard disks susceptible to dirt and damage if moved suddenly. Hard disks can store huge amounts of data.

The files can be read, edited, re-written or deleted. Hard disks are used for storage of the operating system, files and data when not in use at the time or when the computer is turned off.

Solid-state drive (SSD)

SSDs use **flash memory** to store software and data in files. There are no moving parts in SSDs which makes them faster and more reliable than HDDs. They can be more expensive than magnetic hard disks for the same amount of storage so they usually have a smaller capacity than HDDs.

The files can be read, edited, re-written or deleted. They can be used for storage of the operating system, files and data not in use at the time or when the computer is turned off.

Optical device

An optical drive uses **optical media** such as CDs and DVDs to store software and data in files. Blu-ray disks are large capacity optical disks and can store very large amounts of data.

Data stored on CD-ROMS and DVD-ROMs can be read but cannot be altered. The files can be read, edited, re-written or deleted only if CD-R/RWs or DVD-R/RWs are used.

Flash memory devices

Revised

USB memory sticks contain flash memory and are used in **USB** ports. USB memory sticks are used to store data and files for transfer to other computers or for taking away from, or back to, the office.

Cloud storage

Revised

Cloud storage provides very large data storage capacity facilities online for remote access using a web interface. It can be used to easily share files between all members of staff.

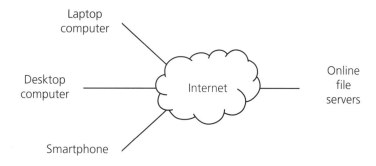

> ### Exam tip
>
> Make sure that you know about the different types of storage and why some are more suitable than others for use in specific computer systems. For example, an HDD is cheaper and has more capacity than an SSD so is used in desktop computers. SSDs are more robust and smaller so are used in tablet computers.

Check your understanding

Tested

17 Explain why a salesperson would store their data on a USB memory stick rather than a DVD-R when transporting files back to the office at the end of a working day.

Go online for answers

Online

Connectivity devices

Network card (NIC)

Revised

A network card is used to connect a computer to a network using a
cable. Connecting a desktop PC to a network uses an **ethernet**
cable.

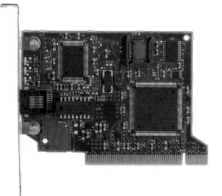

Wireless network card

Revised

A wireless card is used to connect a computer to a network using Wi-Fi/
radio waves. Tablet computers do not normally have a socket for a cable
connection so tablets use wireless NICs. Wireless network cards are also
present in smartphones.

Router

Revised

A router directs network traffic to the correct computer or device and
connects different networks together and to the internet. These are used
to connect a business network to the internet.

Switch

Revised

Switches allow many computers or devices to connect into a network. These are used in large networks to connect devices and to direct network traffic so the network runs efficiently.

Modem

Revised

Modems are used to convert analogue signals to and from digital signals for connection to the internet. They connect laptops or other computers to the internet using ordinary telephone lines – this is a dial up connection.

Wireless Access Point (WAP)

Revised

A **WAP** is used to connect devices to a network using wireless connections/Wi-Fi. It allows laptops or other computing devices, e.g. printers, to use Wi-Fi to connect into an existing network.

> **Exam tip**
>
> You must make sure that you know what each network device does and how it could be used in a business.

Check your understanding

Tested

18 What network device(s) would be required in an office to allow staff to connect a smartphone to a wireless network to access the internet?

Go online for answers

Online

Choosing and configuring systems

Choosing a system

Factors affecting the choice of a business system include the following:

Cost and availability

Business computers are designed to be suitable without costing too much to buy or maintain. Businesses do not typically need very large, high **resolution** monitors or top of the range, high-speed **processors**. Business computers are usually available to buy at any time.

User needs

Business computers must be capable of running office applications at a reasonable speed, store data safely and securely with components that are suitable for long-term use. Some users need monitors that can be rotated to a portrait view.

Data security

Business computers must be capable of storing data so that it is not lost accidentally, through a faulty component (such as hard disk failure) or by being accessed by unauthorised users. Components are chosen for their reliability. Using cheap components is not cost-effective.

Configuring systems

Computers in offices are set up so that the office staff can perform their tasks.

A typical office computer will have:

- a suitable size monitor, a suitable keyboard and mouse, with a hard disk, a DVD/CD re-writer and a network card, with a case to hold the main components
- a windows-based **operating system** such as Microsoft Windows, Apple OS or Linux, with a range of office **applications** such as wordprocessing, desktop publishing, spreadsheet and database software.

Physically impaired workers

Office workers who are physically impaired will have a variety of devices to make their use of a computer easier.

- Puff-suck switches activate switches that select an item on screen or send a command to the computer when the person blows or sucks.

- Braille keyboards have braille markings to allow people with visual impairments to feel the keys and choose one without seeing it.

- A foot mouse is used by feet, instead of hands and fingers, to move the pointer on screen.

Specialised software and settings allow physically impaired people to use computers.

- Text To Speech software reads text aloud and sounds are made, or words are spoken, when commands are entered or carried out.

- Speech To Text software translates spoken commands into actions that the computer carries out and spoken words appear as text in a document.

- Zoom enlarges areas of the screen display as a pointer is moved over the screen.

> **Exam tip**
>
> You must be able to consider the needs of office workers and other employees when choosing the most appropriate computer system for them to use in their jobs and the tasks that they have to carry out.

Check your understanding

19 Why would it be unnecessary to equip every workstation in an administration office of a supermarket with a high performance video gaming computer system?

20 Why would a computer system capable of video-editing be useful in the offices of a leisure centre?

21 Describe how a visually impaired person would be able to create and read emails using specialist hardware and software.

Go online for answers

Using computer systems and devices for remote working

What is remote working? — Revised

People work remotely because they are travelling or work from home.

People working remotely can:

- send emails and transfer files while away from their office
- access their own files over the internet
- access company files stored on company servers or on cloud storage.

How does remote working work? — Revised

The company system that stores the files must be configured to allow remote working access.

The company system must:

- use a router that controls access to a company network and can be set up to allow remote access
- check that the workers have the proper authentication for access by checking the user name and password for the remote user
- be able to send and receive the files securely
- be configured for access to the remote storage.

Remote access can involve:

- sharing the desktop of a computer in the office, which means that the remote computer (a laptop, for instance) appears to be using the desktop as if in the office
- using a virtual private network (VPN) which is a secure connection that appears to be part of the actual company network
- using specialist software such as file transfer protocol (FTP) software for accessing files and folders.

> **Exam tip**
>
> Remote access is useful for employees but can create security problems for the company who owns the network or systems that are remotely accessed. Make sure that you know how these security problems can arise and how they can be prevented and dealt with.

Check your understanding — Tested

22 Describe why each of the following workers would need remote access to a business network:

a) a person selling carpets to businesses for use in their offices

b) a viewer who visits houses that might be for sale

c) an area manager of a chain of supermarkets.

Go online for answers — Online

System software

The operating system:

- manages the hardware
- allows software to be run on the computer for users to carry out tasks.

Operating systems include:

- Android developed by the Open Handset Alliance led by Google, used in smartphones, tablets, netbooks, laptops and desktop computers.
- Apple OS X and iOS
- Linux, which is an open-source operating system used in smartphones, tablets, netbooks, laptops and desktop computers. It has also been used in mobile phones, televisions, TV set-top boxes, routers and video game consoles.
- Microsoft Windows, used in smartphones, tablets, netbooks, laptops and desktop computers.

These operating systems usually have graphical user interfaces (GUIs).

Graphical User Interface (GUI)   Revised ☐

A GUI uses:

- windows to view the task or software in use
- icons or small images to represent the task or choice
- menus to provide choices for the user
- a pointer that can be moved around the screen, e.g. a mouse or touch pad, or on a touch screen using a stylus or fingers.

Utility software   Revised ☐

Utility software or utility tools add extra functions to an operating system or add the ability to carry out technical tasks, such as:

- managing disks
- managing printers
- analysing computer performance
- disk compression and defragmentation
- backups.

Anti-virus and anti-malware software are other examples of utility software.

> **Exam tip**
>
> You must know what software is and what it does. You must also know the different types of software, examples of each and what they do.

Check your understanding   Tested ☐

23 What does GUI stand for?

24 What does the GUI term 'WIMP' stand for?

Go online for answers   Online ☐

Application software

Application software allows users to carry out useful tasks such as writing reports, surfing the web or using email.

Word processors (WP) and desktop publishing software (DTP)

Revised

Word processors and desktop publishing packages are used for writing and producing documents on a personal computer and allow the user to type words and add images to create letters, reports, books, magazines and newspapers.

Desktop publishing software gives the user more control over the layout and where items are placed on pages than word processing software.

Spreadsheet and database management software

Revised

Both spreadsheet and database management software are designed to handle numbers, text and images for processing to provide information for the user.

Spreadsheets:

- have cells in which items of data such as values, labels, titles and formulas are stored
- handle numbers and carry out calculations using functions and formulas
- create graphs to display the data or to show trends in the data.

Databases are used for:

- entry of data
- storage of data
- editing of data
- processing of data by searching and sorting
- retrieval of data.

Databases can be used to store almost any type of data. Databases store data in files made up of records. A record is a collection of fields. A field holds one item of data.

A database can be made of just one table of records – a flat file database – or it may hold many tables of records connected by relationships – a relational database.

Businesses store details of their customers, clients, properties for sale or rent, or stock details in databases.

Presentation, slideshow and multimedia software

Presentation and slideshow software is used to create a series of slides combining text and images.

Slides are shown individually or as part of sequence and are displayed to an audience using a data projector. The presenter can move from one slide to another manually or by setting a timer in the software that changes the slides automatically.

The benefits of using presentation software are:

- the speaker can show text and images
- the slideshow can have links to other media or resources
- the timings of the slideshow can be accurate
- the speaker can pause the show or change the order of slides to suit the audience if manual changes between slides are used
- automatic slide changes can be used so the speaker can talk without having to worry about changing slides
- the slideshow can be used without the speaker being present if automatic slide changes are used.

Multimedia software combines different media sources such as text, images, audio, video, and animations in a presentation.

Multimedia presentations can be linear just as in a cinema or movie, or can have navigation links that allow users a choice of route through a presentation.

Photo-editing and graphics manipulation software

This software has a range of tools and features that are used to create or edit images.

Photographs can:

- be edited to remove red-eye or other unwanted blemishes
- be cropped to remove unwanted parts of the image
- have elements cut off or out of the image
- be resized to fit frames in documents or for use in different devices
- have extra layers created to add new elements to the image.

Video-editing software

Video can be edited to remove unwanted sections, join sections together or add effects such as scene changes, titles or subtitles to improve the final video movie.

Communications software

Revised

Communications software is used for remote access to company networks and to exchange files.

Communications software includes:

- file transfer applications
- instant messaging clients
- email clients
- video and audio 'chat' applications.

Web browsers

Revised

A web browser displays web pages from an intranet or from websites on the internet. Viewers can read text, view images or play video or audio files from the internet using a web browser.

Gaming software

Revised

Gaming software is used to create computer games for others to play. Commercial computer games are created on very powerful computers by many programmers working on different parts alongside each other. The final game is made up of all the programmers' work combined together.

Simpler games can be created on personal computers using freely available software.

Apps for portable devices

Revised

Apps are software applications specially written to make use of the limited memory resources, the touch screen and connectivity found in portable devices.

Apps are available for navigation, accessing email, sending and receiving text messages, viewing web pages, storing photographs, purchasing goods, updating social network pages and many other tasks.

> **Exam tip**
>
> You must be able to explain the tasks that each type of software application is most suitable for. You must be able to explain to others which type of software application they should use for a particular task.

Check your understanding

Tested

25 Explain why a spreadsheet is more suitable for managing financial records than a database.

26 Explain why a database is more suitable for managing the details of club memberships than a spreadsheet.

27 What are 'apps'?

28 What software would be suitable for creating a presentation that contained text, photographs and video? Explain why you chose the software.

29 Describe how a leisure centre receptionist might use photo-editing software.

Go online for answers

Online

How various factors affect the choice of a computer system

The choice of system is affected by:

- cost
- availability
- user needs
- data security.

Choosing a computing device is important because if an unsuitable or too expensive device is chosen the business will not function efficiently or may go out of business altogether.

Cost and availability
Revised

The cost of purchase and maintenance of a computing device in business has to be considered. Businesses often buy computers for users like receptionists and salespeople, with office and communication applications already installed, from suppliers who keep the costs down by supplying them in large quantities.

User needs
Revised

Salespeople and other users who travel and work away from the office use laptops or smartphones for office tasks and communication with other staff and with their employers.

Security
Revised

The security of data stored on a computing device is an important consideration when purchasing and using computers for business. Users must choose secure passwords. The chosen device must make it difficult for others to view data shown on the screen when working in public areas – although users should be advised not to work in public areas at all. Smaller screens, such as those on smartphones or tablets, are more difficult to read at a distance so making it difficult for others to overlook the user.

> **Exam tip**
>
> You must be able to decide on the most suitable computer systems for particular uses and be able to give reasons for your choices.

Check your understanding
Tested

30 The manager of a chain of small shops needs new computers for her own use and for the small group of admin assistants. The assistants work in a office but the manager is often out visiting the shops. Explain why she should buy desktop computers for the admin assistants and a laptop and smartphone for her own use.

Go online for answers
Online

Connecting computer peripherals

What are computer peripherals?

Peripherals are devices attached to, but not actually part of, the main computer system.

Examples are printers, scanners, microphones and **webcams**.

Peripherals can be connected to a computer device by:

● wired methods

● wireless methods.

The most common method of physically connecting a peripheral is to use a USB connection with a cable that plugs into a USB port.

> **Exam tip**
>
> Make sure that you can identify different computer peripherals, how they can be connected and explain their uses.

Physical connections

USB

USB (universal serial bus) is a standard way of connecting devices. USB provides fast data transmission suitable for transferring files such as photographs and is often used between digital cameras and computers.

FireWire

FireWire is a high-speed connection similar to USB and mainly used for connecting storage devices and transferring digital video. FireWire hardware is more expensive than that for USB so is not used so often.

Wireless connections

Wireless connections use radio waves.

Wi-Fi

Wi-Fi is a wireless connection and does not use physical cables. Wireless connections can be complicated to set up, slower to transfer data and may be less secure than cabled connections but are more convenient for the user.

Bluetooth®

Bluetooth® uses wireless technology to connect devices. It is used to connect input devices, such as a mouse, to connect hands-free headsets to a mobile phone and can also be used to exchange data, e.g. photos between mobile phones.

Bluetooth® connections require the devices to be 'paired' using the same password key. They have a limited range.

Wi-Fi and Bluetooth® connections do not need the devices to be in sight of each other.

Infrared connections

Infrared connections need the devices to be very close, usually within one metre. This can make an infra-red connection very safe and secure.

Infrared connections can:

● transfer data between special business cards

● transfer images very quickly.

Exam tip

Make sure that you can explain why different connection methods are used in different situations.

Check your understanding
Tested ☐

31 Why are connections by laptops to the internet made using Wi-Fi and not Bluetooth®?

32 Why is Bluetooth® used between smartphones and hands-free devices in a car instead of Wi-Fi?

Go online for answers
Online ☐

Connecting devices to wireless networks

Wireless connections

Revised

To connect to a wireless network, the computing devices must have a wireless network card. Laptops, tablet computers, smartphones and printers can easily be connected together or to a network using wireless.

The advantages of using wireless networks are:

● avoiding the expense and time of laying network cables to each computer in a building

● connected devices can also be moved around and as long as the device is within range of it will stay connected.

Speed of data transmission

Revised

Wireless networks have slower rates of data transmission than wired networks. The user sees this by having to wait longer for web pages to open, files to download or upload, or by seeing jerky or stuttering playback of videos.

Bandwidth

Revised

The number of devices connected at one time and the **bandwidth** of the connection affect the transfer of large amounts of data over a wireless network connection.

High bandwidth connections allow large amounts of data to be quickly transferred. Watching videos over Wi-Fi requires a high bandwidth connection.

Wireless connections can stop (or drop out) at the edge of the range or if obstacles such as walls are in the way.

Wi-Fi

Revised

Wi-Fi is often used as another name for a wireless network. Public wireless networks (Wi-Fi 'hotspots') allow portable devices to connect to the internet. Wi-Fi hotspots can be found in cafes, hotels, libraries and other public places and have a limited range from the access point.

Service Set Identifier (SSID)

Revised

The Service Set Identifier (SSID) identifies each network by a unique name so that all the devices connected to it can identify the network. It must be used by all the devices on that network if they are to communicate with each other. SSIDs can be set manually by the person who administers the network or set up automatically. Automatic SSID broadcasts can be hidden to make it harder to detect the network. Network administrators can use a public SSID to broadcast to wireless devices in range of an access point.

Security of wireless networks

Revised

Wireless networks can be less secure than wired networks. Potential unauthorised users are not easy to spot and transmitted data can be intercepted by anyone.

Security measures have to be used to prevent data being accessed by unauthorised users.

The data is encrypted using an encryption key often referred to as the 'password', the 'network key' or the 'security key'. Every device has to use the encryption key to connect to, and transfer data over, an encrypted wireless network.

> **Exam tip**
>
> Make sure that you know how to connect a smartphone to a wireless network and why the wireless network asks for a 'key'.

WEP, WPA, WPA2, AES

Revised

WEP (wired equivalent privacy) is an older attempt to secure wireless networks. WPA, WPA2 (Wi-Fi protected access) and AES (advanced encryption standard) have superseded WEP as they are more secure.

Firewall settings

Revised

Firewall settings for devices used on public networks must allow the user of the device access to the internet services needed. However, the firewall should also refuse access to any unauthorised devices to try and prevent, for example, personal data being stolen.

For devices on a private network, firewall settings should allow the device to access and be accessed by other devices on that network so that, for example, scanners or printers can be used. However, the firewall should block attempts to access the private network from unauthorised sources, such as hackers.

Check your understanding

Tested

33 Why does streaming video often pixelate or stop when using a 3G connection?

34 Why is WPA2 used when connecting to a wireless network?

Go online for answers

Online

Remote access to networks

Remote connections

Revised

Staff can connect, using the internet, to their business network when away from their workplace using a Wi-Fi hotspot if remote connections are allowed. This allows staff to do things like update bookings or customer details and use company facilities while away from the workplace on business, e.g. an estate agent viewing a property for rent or working from home.

Remote connections into company networks from the internet pose security dangers. Company networks connect to the internet using a router which can be configured so that only authorised devices and users can access the internet.

Firewalls

Revised

A **firewall** can be configured to allow authorised devices and users and to prevent unauthorised access from the internet to try to protect data stored on the company network.

Firewalls compare the network traffic as it arrives from the internet with rules set by the administrator and, if it is not allowed, will stop the traffic entering the company network.

A firewall will let the user access the network from outside if the rules allow. This can make a company network less secure, so a user ID and password is necessary for remote access.

User ID and password

Revised

A **user ID** and **password** is entered via a web page from the firewall or network to let the user enter the details before being allowed entry to the network.

Staff working remotely will have their laptops or smartphones already configured to use the ID and password so they can access the network remotely.

Hotels allow guests, cafes allow customers and libraries allow visitors to use their wireless networks by providing user IDs and passwords. Entering a correct user ID and password grants the user access to the wireless network and to the internet.

> **Exam tip**
>
> You must make sure that you know about the security issues than arise when using public Wi-Fi hotspots to send confidential documents and to connect to company networks.

Check your understanding

Tested

35 Explain why using a laptop connected to a wireless network in a coffee shop is not good practice when working on confidential documents.

36 Explain why a company network would have a firewall installed.

Go online for answers

Online

Monitoring employees

How organisations can monitor employees

Revised ☐

Organisations can monitor employees by:

- using GPS location tracking
- monitoring internet use and communications.

Organisations want to know what their employees are doing and where they are during their working day because, for instance:

- the police need to know where officers are so that they can be sent to an incident
- a bank will want to know where security staff delivering money to its branches are at all times
- a local council will want to know where its workers are if they are carrying out council duties
- employers have a 'duty of care' to ensure that employees are safe.

Global Positioning System (GPS)

Revised ☐

GPS is a satellite-based system used by GPS receivers to find locations and times anywhere on the surface, or near to the surface, of the Earth.

GPS is free to access by receivers and is used for navigation to or from anywhere that has a line of sight 'view' of four or more of the GPS satellites.

GPS tracking

Revised ☐

GPS tracking uses data from GPS satellites to find the precise location of the GPS tracking device.

A GPS tracking device records its location at set intervals and sends the data using radio, a mobile phone connection or internet connection to a central computer. The location can be stored for later analysis or displayed on a map to 'track' the device in real time.

Uses of GPS tracking

Revised ☐

Company vehicles or laptops can be tracked in this way by fixing a GPS tracking device to the vehicle. People can only be tracked if they carry a GPS tracking device.

Some smartphones have GPS tracking built in but most mobile phones do not have a tracking device even though they have GPS receivers installed. However, the location of a mobile phone can be traced to the nearest mobile phone access point, where it was last connected to the mobile phone system.

Electronic tagging

Revised

Electronic tagging of criminals uses a device that is monitored by a base unit to alert the authorities if the tag goes out of range. Tracking devices used to track criminals do not actively send data about their location. GPS tracking can also be used in some circumstances.

Monitoring internet use and communications

Revised

Companies have a responsibility to ensure that the use of the internet by their employees is appropriate and for the purpose of doing their job.

A member of staff in an office should only use the internet for work purposes and not, for example for booking a personal holiday, for online gambling or playing games. Email use should be for company business and not personal use.

Email monitoring

Revised

To ensure that staff do not abuse the privilege, most companies will scan emails to ensure that no viruses or inappropriate words are included and will keep automatic records and backups of all emails to and from the company systems. Some companies will record telephone conversations to ensure that communications are appropriate.

Most companies let their staff use the email and internet for private use provided they do not abuse the privilege and bring the company into disrepute.

Company policy

Revised

Most companies have a policy about tracking the use of the internet and recording telephone calls by employees.

Employees should be informed that the company is monitoring their use of the internet and communications. The company must inform a caller to the company that the call may be recorded.

Exam tip

Make sure that you understand why businesses would want to track the activities and locations of their employees and how this could be done. Also, make sure that you know about the ethical implications of the tracking.

Check your understanding

Tested

37 How could an employee's smartphone be used to track the communications and location of a salesperson who visits homes to measure rooms for new carpets?

Go online for answers

Online

Data

Data types

Revised

You must consider the type of data to be stored, and how it is to be stored and used before data is entered into, for example, a spreadsheet or database. The different types of data are shown below.

Data type	Description	Example of data	Typical use
Text	Any character	XY|<.<;;65 3	Names of items
Integer number	Whole numbers	192	Number of people in a shop
Real numbers	Numbers with decimal places	12.99	Prices, height, weight
Date	Time	26/03/1969	A date, e.g. 26th March 1969
Boolean	True or False	Only two choices: 1 or 0, yes or no, M or F	Storing a person's gender
Image	A graphic file	A photograph	A photograph on a membership card

Text can be used to store any type of data. Calculations cannot be carried out on data stored as text but it can be sorted and searched.

Telephone 'numbers' are stored as text because they can have spaces, dashes and leading zeroes.

If calculations are required on data, such as currency and dates, they have to be stored as numbers.

Exam tip

You must make sure that you know the most appropriate data type for particular pieces of data.

Data capture methods

Revised

Data is collected for many reasons. The choice of method of capturing the data will depend on why it is needed and how it is to be used.

- DJs requesting songs to play on their radio programme could use instant messaging, social networks or email to allow the audience to send song suggestions.
- Recording the votes in an election could be done with paper voting sheets or online forms.

Coding data

Revised

To save space in a spreadsheet or database file, data can be coded.

Examples of coding of data include:

- Y or N instead of Yes or No
- M or F instead of male or female
- Mr instead of Mister
- Dr instead of Doctor.

Every item in a stock database is given a code that can be searched for or sorted into order. Data such as 'red, large sofa with arms' is more complicated than a code such as S_ARL and takes longer to process.

Making sure that data is accurate

Revised

Data stored in a spreadsheet or database must be accurate as it is used to retrieve useful information.

There are two methods of ensuring data is accurate: verification and validation. Neither method makes sure that the data is correct; only that it is entered accurately and is the right sort of data.

Verification

Revised

Verification checks that data is entered exactly as it is shown on the original data capture sheet. Verification can be done by:

- a visual check – to see if the data in the computer system is the same as that on the original questionnaire
- double entry – data is entered twice, by different operators, for large amounts of data, so the computer system can check one set against the other. If any differences are found, the computer system will report the differences to the operators.

Double entry can also be used, for instance, when the same individual enters a new password into an online form.

Validation

Revised

Validation uses rules to make sure that data is reasonable and abides by the rules set up when, for example the spreadsheet or database was created. Validation checks the data as it is entered to ensure that the data is allowed into the system.

Validation checks include:

- presence check – ensures that data is actually entered by the user
- data type check – ensures that the data is the correct type
- format or picture check – ensures that the data is in the correct format
- range check – ensures that the data is within set limits
- character check – ensures that only allowed characters can be entered and others are rejected.

Other validation checks can be made on data. For example, a check digit is a digit added to a bar code and is a number calculated from the bar code digits. When the digits are read from the bar code the check digit is calculated again to make sure that they have been read accurately.

Exam tip

Make sure that you know why different validation checks are necessary when entering data into a database.

Check your understanding

Tested

1 Why are telephone numbers stored as text in databases?

2 Why is some data coded for storage in a database?

3 Why are validation checks necessary when data is being entered into a database?

Go online for answers

Online

How data is captured

Nature of information

Revised ☐

A number of factors affect how data is captured.

The nature and type of the information to be collected will determine the way it is collected, for example:

● names, addresses and post codes are text

● height and weight are numbers.

How is data captured?

Revised ☐

Collecting **data** and **information** for use in computer systems can be carried out:

● manually using paper-based

● automatically using online forms

● using automated data capture systems with sensors such as temperature sensors or bar code readers.

> **Exam tip**
>
> Data is letters, numbers and characters without meaning. Information is data that has been processed and given meaning and a context.

Data capture forms

Revised ☐

Data has to be collected in a suitable format so that it can be easily entered into a computer and then processed to provide the information required.

Online forms are used to enter data directly into computer systems, often over the internet using websites. This method of data capture is useful for collecting the details of new customers or prospective clients by, for example an estate agent or a leisure centre.

Data capture forms are pre-printed forms with questions and spaces for the answers, such as questionnaires. Online forms are similar.

Paper-based forms are often filled out by a member of staff who asks questions and then writes the answers onto the form. The questions and spaces on the form should be designed to get specific data from the customer or client which is then transcribed into a computer system. Most forms show examples of how data should be entered.

PLEASE COMPLETE IN CAPITAL LETTERS ONLY

Mr ☐   Mrs ☐   Miss ☐   Ms ☐

First Name: ☐☐☐☐☐☐☐☐☐☐☐☐☐☐☐☐☐☐
Surname: ☐☐☐☐☐☐☐☐☐☐☐☐☐☐☐☐☐☐
Address: ☐☐☐☐☐☐☐☐☐☐☐☐☐☐☐☐☐☐
☐☐☐☐☐☐☐☐☐☐☐☐☐☐☐☐☐☐☐
☐☐☐☐☐☐☐☐☐☐☐☐☐☐☐☐☐☐☐
Postcode: ☐☐☐☐   ☐☐☐
D.O.B.: ☐☐ ☐☐ ☐☐
Mobile: ☐☐☐☐☐☐☐☐☐☐☐
Home Tel: ☐☐☐☐☐☐☐☐☐☐☐
Email: _____

Employee Details

* Employee Id [＿＿＿＿＿＿＿＿]

* First Name [＿＿＿＿＿＿＿＿]

* Last Name [＿＿＿＿＿＿＿＿]

* Email [＿＿＿＿＿＿＿＿]

Phone number [＿＿＿＿＿＿＿＿]

Salary [＿＿＿＿＿＿＿＿]

Department [＿＿＿＿＿＿▼]

[Save]   *Required

Designing data capture forms

Revised

Designers of data capture forms should consider:

- having a set number of spaces for an answer to guide the person filling in the form
- specifying the type of answer to be accepted to make sure that the data is collected in a suitable format
- collecting data such as temperature as numbers so analysis can be carried out
- collecting names as text so that any character can be used
- giving guidance and instructions for people filling in the forms – this is especially important for paper forms where people can write anything.
- the environment in which, or from which, the data is to be collected.

Online data capture forms can limit the type of data entered to make sure that data that is entered by the user is in the correct format, for example using:

- **drop down menus** to force a single choice from a pre-set selection of choices
- **boxes** to force a yes or no response
- a **single character text box** for each letter of a name
- a **pre-set format** for a date so that all forms are completed in the same way
- **radio buttons** forcing a single choice from several options
- **validation rules** to make sure that the data meets specific requirements or that all specific questions have to be answered before the user can move to the next question.

Designers of data capture forms should avoid:

- using small fonts that are difficult to read
- using small boxes for writing or typing
- not having enough boxes or having too many boxes
- asking vague questions
- not specifying the format for data entry that is required
- using overlapping choices to collect data about, for example the number of times a person has used a website. The ranges should not be 0–5, 5–10, 10–15 because the ranges overlap.
- using a single text box to collect an address, making it very difficult to sort or search when stored on a computer system.

Data Collection Sheet

Please check that the information below Is correct.

Surname [   ]   Forename [   ]
Middle Name (s) [   ]
Gender [▼]   Date of birth [Day ▼] [Month ▼] [Year ▼]
Address [   ]
Post code [   ]

Please give details of all persons who have parental responsibility and anyone else you wish to be contacted in an emergency.

Place them in the order you wish them to be contacted in an emergency.

Name	Relationship	Address	Contact number

Travel details   Please tick appropriate choice

Bicycle ⚪   Train⚪   Bus ⚪   Walk⚪   Car⚪   Taxi⚪   Other [   ]

Check your understanding

Tested

4   When using a paper form, why is it preferable to collect a person's date of birth by asking them to fill in dd/mm/yyyy rather than asking the person to write their date of birth on a blank line?

Go online for answers

Online

Paper forms and online forms

Paper forms for collecting data are given to people so that they can fill them in and return them. Leisure centres would use a paper form so that it can be given to a new member to complete while the receptionist carries on with other tasks.

Paper forms that are filled in, for example at a leisure centre, can be used to collect data, such as the names of new members.

Using paper forms to collect information from people can be costly because of the cost of:

● the paper and printing
● the time taken by the person asking the questions
● the time for the person transcribing the data from the paper form into the computer system
● the time taken to check that the data has been entered accurately.

The data written on paper forms may:

● be hard to read if the handwriting is not clear
● be incomplete, or may be wrong if the user does not answer truthfully.

Online forms can be used to collect data such as the names and addresses of prospective customers for supermarket online shopping.

Online data capture forms are always clear to read as the answers are typed or coded in boxes. Rules can be set up to make sure all the data is entered but there is nothing an online form can do to make a user answer truthfully.

> **Exam tip**
>
> You must be able to consider the type and nature of data that is being collected and use this to decide how best to collect it in specific circumstances.

Check your understanding — Tested

5 Why would a receptionist who is signing up a new member of a leisure centre use an online form to collect details rather than give the member a paper form to complete?

Go online for answers — Online

Automated data capture

Automated data capture systems
Revised

Data is captured automatically to controll an air conditioning system or when selling goods at a supermarket checkout, for instance. Data about physical parameters is collected by sensors.

- Temperature sensors measure the temperature of a room for use in a heating/air conditioning system or the temperature of freezer cabinets in shops, for example.
- pH sensors measure the pH of a swimming pool for use in water quality control systems.
- Light sensors measure the light level in a room for use in controlling lighting systems.
- Pressure sensors measure the water pressure in a central heating system.

Exam tip

You must be able to explain how the data from sensors can be used by businesses in the everyday running of their operations. For instance, how temperature data is used by supermarkets to monitor the condition of their freezers in store.

Analogue and digital data
Revised

Data collected by sensors is in analogue form and has to be converted to digital form for use by computer systems. Sensors are connected via an **analogue to digital converter** to a computer which can record or use the data.

Exam tip

You must be able to choose the most appropriate sensor for a specific use.

Bar codes
Revised

All goods for sale in supermarkets have bar codes which contain data that can uniquely identify the item. The bar code is read by a bar code scanner/reader at the checkout and the data is read and used to look up the details of the item in a database on the supermarket's computer system.

Self-service checkouts work because all the information about the item does not need to be entered again since it is already on the store database. The customer scans the bar code and the details are retrieved and displayed on the screen.

Staff also use hand-held or portable readers to:

- scan the items on the shelves
- count the number of items on the shelf
- send the data to the store computer system to update the database so the store knows how many items are in stock.

Matrix bar codes

Revised

Matrix bar codes (two-dimensional bar codes) are often called QR codes (quick response codes). They carry more data than a conventional bar code.

The code is made up of black modules arranged in a square pattern on a white background and can be read much faster than ordinary bar codes.

QR codes can be read by a smartphone using a free app. This allows the user to be given more information about the product very quickly and to link directly to the manufacturer or retailer website.

RFID tags

Revised

Radio Frequency Identification (RFID) tags are small devices which use radio waves to transfer data from the tag to a computer system. RFID tags are used by supermarkets to automatically identify items.

Near field communications

Revised

Near field communications (NFC) are used in smartphones to create radio links over a very short range of a few centimetres or less.

A smartphone using NFC is touched or waved very close to another device to:

● exchange data such as a configuration for Wi-Fi

● make contactless financial transactions, e.g. pay for parking

● fast data transfer of transaction details similar to those in credit cards to allow 'mobile payment'.

NFC sets itself up faster than Bluetooth® and there is no need for pairing, but data transfer is slower than Bluetooth®.

Check your understanding

Tested

6 Explain how the data needed to control an air conditioning system is collected automatically by a computer system?

7 Why would temperature and pH sensors be used to collect data from a leisure centre's swimming pool?

Go online for answers

Online

File formats

Files created by software applications, using different **file formats**, are stored on storage media so that they can be retrieved for use later. Operating systems use file formats to decide which application to use to open the file. Some operating systems use file extensions to show the file format while others look inside the file to find out what type of file is being accessed. Microsoft Windows uses file extensions.

Proprietary formats

Proprietary formats are those owned and used by commercial companies.

Format file extension	Meaning	Typically used to store
.doc .docx	Microsoft Word document	Word-processed letters
.xls .xlsx	Microsoft Excel document	Spreadsheets
.ppt .pptx	Microsoft PowerPoint document	Slideshow presentations
.fla	Adobe Flash movie/animation	Animations/movies
.wma	Windows media audio	Audio/sounds

Open formats

Open formats are those formats that others are allowed to use. A variety of software applications use open formats and they can be used to transfer data between applications. Some open file formats are shown below.

Format file extension	Meaning	Typically used to store
.aac	Advanced audio coding	Audio/sounds stored without loss of data
.rtf	Rich text format	Word-processed documents
.csv	Comma separated values	Lists of data
.exe	Executable file	Applications that can be run on computer systems
.txt	Text	Text files
.pdf	Portable document format	Formatted documents
.mp3	MPEG audio layer 3	Audio/sounds stored with loss of data when the file is compressed
.aiff	Apple's audio format	Audio/sounds
.wav	Microsoft's audio format used by many computer systems	Audio/sounds

Choosing an appropriate file format

The choice of file format to use depends upon:

- the file contents
- how best to store the contents
- which software application has created the file
- how the user intends to use the file.

The contents of a file may be video, audio, images, text, or numbers which have to be stored in a way that ensures that the data can be retrieved and used again at a later date.

A DTP file saved on a computer disk will contain text, numbers and images which have to be linked so that they are in the correct place when the file is opened again.

The person creating a file using Microsoft's Publisher application would normally choose to save it as a 'publisher' file but may choose one of the others, for instance:

- PDF which can be opened by free PDF readers on most computers and mobile devices, e.g. smartphones
- plain text – only the text is stored properly
- rich text format for transferring the document to other computing devices and applications
- web page formats used on a website
- PostScript format used for printing purposes.

Choosing a file format for saving an image is important as most image file formats compress the image and this may lose some of the details.

Files that are intended to be shared should be saved in a format that most, if not all, computers and portable devices can use.

Sharing files over the internet will influence the choice of format because very large files can take a very long time to send or receive.

> **Exam tip**
>
> File types are important because they describe what the file contains and tell the operating system what application is used to open the file.

Check your understanding

8 What file type would be best for saving a document that is to be posted on the internet and then opened in many different types of computer system?

9 Why would a music composer store her files as .aac files rather than .mp3 files?

Go online for answers

Data security

What is data security?

Revised

Data must be kept safe and secure from loss or accidental damage when being stored or transmitted by computing devices.

Keeping the data safe means preventing it from being accidentally lost or damaged.

Keeping the data secure means preventing unauthorised users from accessing the data.

Data can be kept safe by:

- saving work regularly
- never working on the only copy of the work
- shutting down the computer properly
- storing storage media such as CDs and other removable media carefully.

Data can be kept secure by:

- physically protecting the data
- encrypting the data
- using passwords to control access to the data.

Many organisations use backups and secure storage methods to safeguard their data by using passwords for access and by encrypting stored or transmitted data. The proper use of backups can also help to keep data safe and secure.

> **Exam tip**
> Ensure that you can describe how data can be kept safe and secure.

Access rights and permissions

Revised

All files and folders have **access rights** and **permissions** to control who can read, edit and save the file.

Organisations can control which files people are allowed to look at by setting different access permissions to the file.

Files and folders can be protected by setting the access rights to read-only so that the files cannot be altered. Individual documents can have passwords set so that only authorised staff can open the file to read and/or edit the contents.

Passwords can be set on whole documents or parts of the document only. For example, in spreadsheets an office worker may be allowed to enter data about prices but not be allowed to change the formulas.

Physical security

Revised

Physical security can be:

- using security guards to protect the physical goods in supermarkets
- posting guards at the doors of offices where the computers are used or at the doors of the rooms where the data is stored on the computer servers
- locking the doors and only giving keys to staff who are allowed to enter the area
- having electronic security locks that need a code to open
- using RFID tags in staff badges to keep out unauthorised people
- not having the computer systems on the ground floor with windows that can be broken to gain access
- facing computer screens away from windows, doors and walkways to stop people seeing what is being displayed
- having bars or strengthened glass on windows and doors
- having strong doors.

Security badges

Revised

Badges with RFID tags can be used to control where staff are allowed to access. Changing the data on the RFID tag will allow staff access to different areas.

Encryption

Revised

Encryption software uses an **encryption code** or **key** to scramble (encrypt) the contents of data files. The proper code is needed to unscramble the file (decrypt it) so it can be read and used. The data is meaningless if the encrypted file is accessed by anyone without the proper code.

Data can be scrambled using **encryption software** when it is stored or transmitted between computers over networks.

Digital signatures are used to check that a website or a message is authentic and are an example of encryption in use.

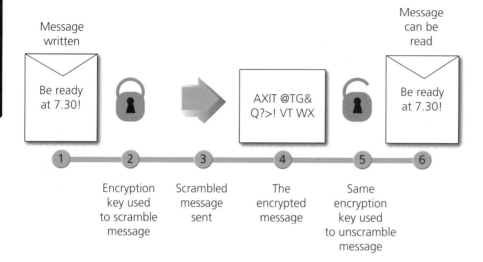

Message written

Be ready at 7.30!

AXIT @TG& Q?>! VT WX

Be ready at 7.30!

Message can be read

1   2   3   4   5   6

Encryption key used to scramble message

Scrambled message sent

The encrypted message

Same encryption key used to unscramble message

Secure websites
Revised

Data should be encrypted before being transmitted when customers buy goods or use services online. Everyone should check that the website uses encryption when entering personal details.

A secure website will show a small padlock and will use **https** instead of **http** in the URL to show that it is using encryption.

Check your understanding
Tested

10 Why is encrypted data of no use to people without an encryption key?

11 What does https stand for and why is it used?

Go online for answers
Online

Data transferring technologies

Data can be transferred between computing devices by networking the devices together.

Internet Revised

The internet is a very large, global network using public telecommunications to which other networks can be connected to transfer data between networks.

Almost anyone can use the internet so any data transferred over the internet is not very secure.

Connecting networks Revised

Networks are used to transfer data between computing devices.

Networks can be connected using cables (wires) that go to each computing device. There is a hub, switch or router to which all the devices such as desktop computers, servers and printers connect. Wired networks can work at very high speeds.

Wired networks can be expensive to set up as the cost of installation and cables can be high for large networks. The cables can be difficult to place in older buildings and may be unsightly in homes.

Wireless networks use radio waves to connect devices via a wireless access point and are easy to set up. However, they can be complex to configure and make secure. Portable devices such as smartphones and laptops have built-in wireless network cards and can easily connect to a wireless network. The devices can be moved around and used anywhere in range of a wireless access point but the speed is usually slower than wired networks.

> **Exam tip**
> You must know about the different ways to transfer data between computers and about the benefits and drawbacks of each method.

Connecting while mobile or travelling Revised

Many hotels, cafes and shops offer free wireless networking to their guests and customers but some make a high charge for its use.

Mobile phones, smartphones and other portable devices can use the mobile phone telecommunication networks, called 3G or 4G networks, to connect to networks and the internet. 3G or 4G networks offer much slower speeds than wired or wireless networks. 4G networks have a greater bandwidth than 3G networks.

Emails Revised

Emails are sent from a device such as a smartphone to an email server which sends the emails to other servers and then to the email inbox of the recipient.

Email was originally designed for sending simple messages but it is now possible to attach files such as photographs, documents and video for sharing with others.

File sharing

Files can be shared by using a file server. The file is uploaded to the server where it is stored until another person downloads it and opens it.

Peer-to-peer file sharing is used to transfer a file directly from one device to another without using a file server.

Cloud computing

Cloud computing is online file storage. Users do not know exactly where the servers are based and only access their files on the servers over the internet.

The company hosting the file servers is responsible for ensuring that the data is kept safe and secure. This type of storage can be cost-effective for smaller businesses that do not have their own servers.

Data transfer speeds

More data can be transferred in a set time over wired networks than wireless networks so wired networks are usually faster than wireless networks.

Bandwidth

Bandwidth is measured in bits per second. High-speed networks will have bandwidths of megabits per second – millions of bits per second. The available bandwidth will determine how fast a file such as a video or audio file can be downloaded. 3G mobile connections are just about good enough for streaming video but 4G mobile connections are much better because of the greater bandwidth available with 4G connections.

File compression

Compressing digital video and audio files to make them small enough to be streamed over low bandwidth connections allows them to be played on smartphones and other portable devices. However, highly-compressed video and audio is poor quality and only suitable for small devices.

> **Exam tip**
>
> Make sure that you know why bandwidth and data compression techniques are important when transferring files over the internet.

Router technology

Routers transmit data round networks. High speeds are achieved by the use of copper and fibre cables or, in the case of wireless routers, by the use of different frequency bands being combined together to increase bandwidth.

Optimisation of files

Files are optimised for transfer to give short download times or faster streaming of the video or audio. Optimisation of video and audio files usually involves reducing the frame rate, reducing the dimensions of the video frame and compressing the audio by changing the sampling rate.

Check your understanding

12 What is the internet?

13 Why do companies connect their computing devices in a network?

14 Why are 4G networks more suitable than 3G networks for use when watching streamed video?

Go online for answers

Factors affecting the choice of data transfer method

What can affect the choice of data transfer method?

Factors that affect the choice of method of data transfer between computing devices include:

- the size of the file holding the data
- the type of data in the file
- the location of the data and the destination of the data
- how quickly the user wants the data to arrive at its destination
- the security of the data
- the needs of the user, e.g. what the user wants to do with the data
- what the data may be used for, and how it might be stored and processed in the future.

USB memory sticks or re-writable CD/DVDs can be used to transfer files between computers that are close together or can be easily visited. These are quite cheap and quick to use and secure as long as they are not lost and the data is deleted once transfer is complete.

Email can be used to transfer files by using attachments but there is often a limit on the size of file that can be sent by email. Email is not secure so data should be encrypted.

Networks can be used to transfer files conveniently and often quickly, even when very large. File transfer is often faster over wired networks than over wireless networks due to the higher bandwidth available. Wireless networks are not as secure as wired networks so private or confidential data may be at risk when being transferred over wireless networks if it is not encrypted.

Security of data is an important consideration when carrying around USB memory sticks, CDs or DVDs as these can be easily lost or stolen. CDs and DVDs can also be scratched or damaged with the result that data is lost.

Exam tip

Make sure that you know the reasons why businesses use different data transfer methods for sending confidential documents to suppliers or customers, or for transferring small files within businesses.

Make sure you know why some methods of data transfer are not suitable.

Check your understanding

15 Why might people use USB memory sticks rather than re-writable CDs to transfer files between computers?

16 Why do some businesses forbid their employees to send confidential information by email?

17 Why does the transfer of large files seem quicker over wired networks than over wireless networks?

Go online for answers

Backups

Backups are copies of data or files that are currently in use.

Archives are copies of data or files that are no larger needed for day-to-day use.

Data and files kept for backup and archive purposes by businesses should be encrypted.

Creating backups in organisations

Backups are created by making encrypted copies of important files.

Large capacity, but expensive, tape drives and extra hard disks are used to store the backups and archives of large companies.

Backups created by organisations are encrypted and protected from theft or fire.

Many smaller businesses pay external companies for the use of 'cloud storage' or online backup services because using their own tape drives or additional hard disks is expensive. The cost is less than having to pay for in-house backup systems.

Backup frequency for businesses

Businesses make backup copies of data and files at a set time every day after the day's work has been done. This is often during the night when employees are not using the system. Banks make backups every few minutes because their financial data is so important.

Smaller businesses do not need to make backups as often as banks but should do so each day.

Using **removable media** for backups or archives means that the media can be stored safely and securely, usually in a different building in a locked area away from the computer systems. Backups and archives of data should also be encrypted.

Exam tip

Make sure that you can explain why backups are necessary and how they can be used in the event of files being lost.

Creating backups at home

Home users should also make backups at regular intervals so they do not lose valuable data such as documents or photographs.

Backups of data from home computers can be made onto removable media such as writable CDs or DVDs or USB flash memory sticks. Removable media used at home only have a small capacity and can be easily lost.

People should be advised not to work on the original copy of any file in case it is corrupted in use or some of it is accidentally deleted.

Why make backups at home and at school

Home users should make backups of important files and in schools, it is important to make backups of school work in case it gets deleted or corrupted in use.

Incremental backups

Backup systems can create copies of only the data that is new or that has changed since the last time a backup was created, saving media space and time. Incremental backups can be used to restore the latest data and files quite quickly.

A backup restores the data, file or disk to the state it was in when the backup was made so the most recent work may still be lost.

Recovering data or files using a backup

A **disk image** takes a snapshot of the whole disk including the operating system and can be used to re-create the whole disk contents.

A backup can be used to restore original files or data by copying the backup data or file back into the original place. Many backup systems allow individual files to be accessed and restored without the need for a full restoration of the whole system.

Archives

Archives are collections of data that are needed but no longer in everyday use.

Archives can be made in the same way as backups – copies of whole disks or of individual files that are stored safely. Archived data is removed from the computer system. For backups, the original data is not removed because it is still needed for everyday use.

Archived data has to be kept so that it can be used for reference in case the information is needed, for instance, for tax purposes or to contact an ex-employee or ex-student.

> **Exam tip**
>
> Make sure that you can explain the difference between a backup and an archive.

Check your understanding

18 Why do banks make backups of their files so often?

19 What is meant by an incremental backup?

20 What is meant by a disk image?

Go online for answers

Factors affecting the choice of backup method

Comparing different methods of backup
Revised

Type of method used for backup	Cost	Ease of use	Data security
Tape system	Expensive	• New tape needed every backup • Tapes susceptible to damage	• Data is encrypted • Tapes are small in size so easily stolen or lost
Additional hard disks in a dedicated server	Expensive	• Data has to be transferred to separate server	• Encrypted data is transferred over network • Disks not easily stolen
External hard disks	Relatively cheap to use	• USB connections not on all devices and data transfers can be slow	• The disks can be easily damaged, lost or stolen • Data can be encrypted
Writable CDs and DVDs	Media is cheaper than hard disks but may be more expensive if large quantities are needed	• New CDs or DVDs needed every time • Not enough for large organisations to create full backups • Suitable for home use	• Media easily stolen or lost
USB memory sticks	Cheap to buy	• Will work in almost all computer systems that have USB connections for external memory sticks	• Most USB memory sticks have the facility to encrypt the data stored on them

Exam tip
It is important that you can explain why a particular type of backup method would be chosen by a specific business.

Check your understanding
Tested

21 Why would a home user choose to make backups on DVD-Rs and not with a tape system?

22 Why are USB memory sticks often chosen by home users to keep copies of their files?

Go online for answers
Online

Communication methods and how they support businesses

Business communication needs
Revised

Businesses need to use reliable and fast communication methods. These will enable the business, and its employees, to work effectively.

Customers will also need to be communicated with to ensure that, for example, they are aware of any special offers, new products or services being offered which will help to keep customer loyalty.

As technology, including the internet, has improved, there have been many developments in communication methods.

> **Exam tip**
>
> You should be able to describe communication methods and how they can assist a business to increase the effectiveness of communications.
>
> You should be able to apply your knowledge to a given scenario.

Communication methods
Revised

A business can use a range of communication methods. The method used must be appropriate for the person receiving the information and the information being sent.

Method	Description
Voice telephones	Can be fixed land line or mobile and enable people to talk to each other. A land line can only receive calls where the phone is located but a mobile call can be taken at any location as long as there is a signal.
SMS (Short Message Service)	A system that lets mobile phone users send and receive text messages.
Instant messaging (IM)	The exchange of typed messages between computer users in real time via the internet.

(Continued)

Method	Description
Email (electronic mail) 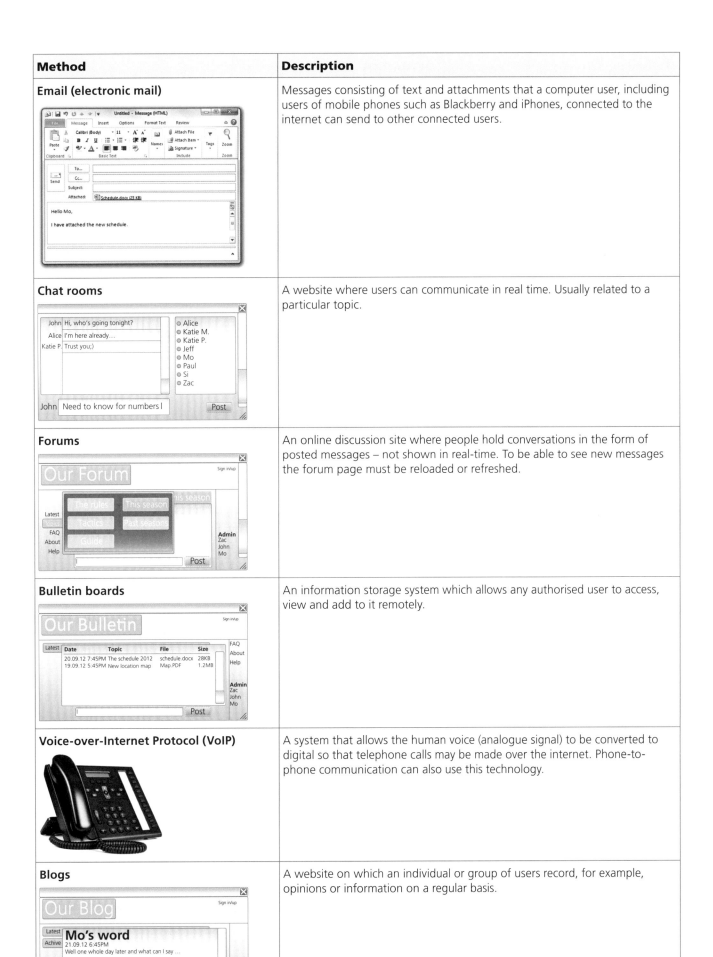	Messages consisting of text and attachments that a computer user, including users of mobile phones such as Blackberry and iPhones, connected to the internet can send to other connected users.
Chat rooms	A website where users can communicate in real time. Usually related to a particular topic.
Forums	An online discussion site where people hold conversations in the form of posted messages – not shown in real-time. To be able to see new messages the forum page must be reloaded or refreshed.
Bulletin boards	An information storage system which allows any authorised user to access, view and add to it remotely.
Voice-over-Internet Protocol (VoIP)	A system that allows the human voice (analogue signal) to be converted to digital so that telephone calls may be made over the internet. Phone-to-phone communication can also use this technology.
Blogs	A website on which an individual or group of users record, for example, opinions or information on a regular basis.

(Continued)

Method	Description
Videoconferencing 	The conduct of a videoconference allows two or more locations to communicate by simultaneous two-way video and audio transmissions.
Webcams	A video camera that inputs to a computer connected to the internet, so that live streaming of images can be viewed by internet users.
Social networking 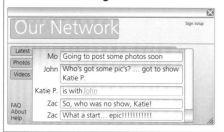	The use of a dedicated website to communicate informally with other members of the site, by posting, for example, messages, photographs or videos.

Check your understanding

Tested ☐

1 Describe how a mobile phone can help a business to contact an employee who works remotely.

2 Describe how email could be used to contact customers with marketing material.

3 Describe how a bulletin board could be used by a business to increase communication between employees.

Go online for answers

Online ☐

Advantages and disadvantages of communication methods

Each communication method has benefits and drawbacks to a business, employees and customers.

Method	Benefits	Drawbacks
Voice telephones	• Voice conversations can be held at a fixed (land lines) or any geographic (mobiles) location. • Voicemail messages can be left.	• The phone signal for a mobile may be weak or down so calls cannot be taken. • Land line phones may not always be answered. • Time differences may not be considered when making a call to a mobile phone.
SMS	• It's cheap – usually included in mobile phone packages. • Short messages can be sent. • The location of the mobile phone does not matter.	• Only short messages can be sent. • Can be difficult to type an SMS on a phone key pad. • May not be delivered if the phone network is down.
Instant messaging	• Messages and responses are sent in real time. • Files/pictures can be sent. • It is possible to talk to many people at once.	• Emotions cannot be expressed as well as they can be when actually talking to a person. • People can send viruses through files/pictures.
Email	• Information can be sent quickly to many people at the same time. • Attachments can be sent. • Can be accessed using a range of devices as long as there is access to the internet. • Employees'/customers' email addresses can be stored.	• Email can become impersonal or misunderstood. • Emails may get sent to the wrong person if addresses are not checked. • People may not receive emails because of no internet connection/filters on email settings. • Attachments can contain a virus. • Email accounts can get hacked with spam being sent to all contacts.
Chat rooms	• Brings people together who have an interest in a specific topic. • Users may not have the opportunity to interact in the real world due to, for example, remote location.	• Information provided by users may be false/untrue. • You don't know who you are talking to. • Can be very addictive.
Forums	• Ideas can be shared between users. • Posts/threads can be read and reread.	• They can be time consuming to maintain and monitor. • Comments/posts are not available in real time.
Bulletin boards	• Any registered user can make comments which are visible to everyone immediately. • Can get a fast response to a question/comment. • For general discussion on topics, interesting and useful comments can be given.	• Any registered user can make comments/answers which may be wrong. • Needs to be moderated by a responsible/trustworthy person.
Voice-over-Internet Protocol (VoIP)	• With a broadband internet connection (DSL or cable), PC-to-PC phone calls are free. • Calls can be made wherever there is a broadband connection by signing in to the VoIP account. • Lots of features such as call forwarding, call waiting, voicemail, caller ID and three-way calling. • Data can be sent at the same time as the call is being made. • Some services also allow videoconferencing.	• PC to voice phone calls can be costly. • No service during a power cut. • Poor or limited internet connection can affect the quality of the call. • Using a PC at the same time can reduce the quality of the call.

(Continued)

Method	Benefits	Drawbacks
Blogs	<ul><li>They are an easy way to keep people updated on a project.</li><li>Can be used as marketing tools by businesses and to get customer/employee feedback.</li></ul>	<ul><li>Need to be moderated which can take a lot of time.</li><li>Posts are not private and information could be 'leaked'.</li></ul>
Videoconferencing	<ul><li>People don't need to travel so costs can be reduced.</li><li>Better for environment.</li><li>People taking part can be at different locations.</li><li>Videoconferencing can be carried out using VoIP services.</li></ul>	<ul><li>Time zones may be different in different parts of the world.</li><li>The equipment can fail or systems may crash/go offline.</li><li>Training may be needed to use the equipment or someone may need to be employed to set up and maintain the equipment.</li><li>To take part everyone must have the equipment.</li></ul>
Webcams	<ul><li>Used to carry out a videoconference.</li><li>Allows realtime and face-to-face personal interaction.</li><li>Allows people around the country or world to see and communicate.</li><li>Can reduce travel expenses.</li><li>Allows projects to be monitored in realtime and objects/charts can be shown.</li></ul>	<ul><li>Can be expensive to buy if advanced features are needed.</li><li>Does not fully show human reactions to what is being said or shown.</li></ul>
Social networking	<ul><li>A business can upload pictures/files to promote their business and increase awareness.</li><li>A business can 'follow' their competitors to see what they are doing.</li></ul>	<ul><li>Lack of anonymity – some users may post too many personal details so affecting work and private life.</li><li>Can be time-consuming and detract from 'normal' life.</li><li>Scams and identity theft can occur.</li></ul>

Exam tip

You will need to be able to describe the benefits and drawbacks of different communication methods.

You will also need to apply these to a business, its employees and customers.

Check your understanding

Tested

4 Describe two benefits to the customers of a business of being contacted by email.

5 Describe one drawback, relating to equipment, of the use of videoconferencing.

6 Describe one benefit and one drawback of the use of mobile telephones to communicate with employees.

7 Describe two benefits to a business of using VoIP as a communication method.

Go online for answers

Online

Email and email etiquette

Email

Revised

Email can be a very clear method of communication. Emails must be used appropriately if the message is to be useful to the person receiving it.

An email is made up of two parts – the header and the body.

The **body** is the main contents of the email. The **header** contains:

- From: the email address of the sender of the email
- To: the email address(es) of the person(s) the email is being sent to
- Subject: a brief summary of the contents of the email
- Date: the time and date the email was sent
- Attachment: where any files are shown.

> **Exam tip**
>
> You should know about the different features of emails, how they can be used and their benefits and drawbacks.

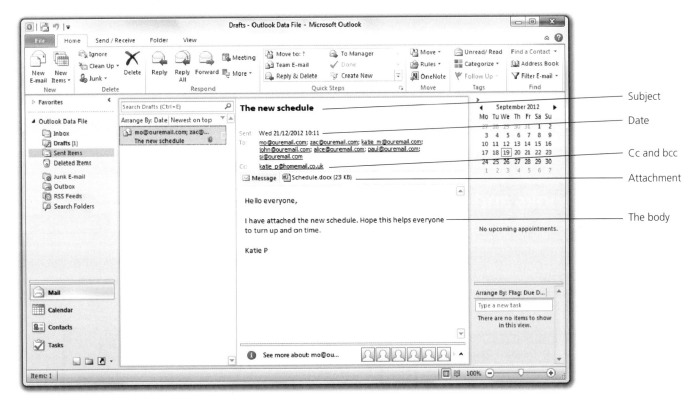

The business should make sure that the information in the header of the email is correct and appropriate.

Subject

Revised

A **subject line** should always be included as it gives the person receiving the email an idea of what the email is about. It should be meaningful, giving a description of what the email is about. If no subject is given then a spam filter will consider it to be 'junk email' and it may be deleted or moved to a junk email box and automatically deleted. This would be bad for a business as it means that the email would not be read.

Cc and bcc

Revised

Addresses placed in the **cc** (carbon copy) line mean everyone who is sent the email will receive it and is able to see who else was sent the email.

Addresses placed in the **bcc** (blind carbon copy) are like cc but the people who were sent the email will not be shown. Can be used:

- if an email needs to be sent to lots of people but the sender does not want email addresses to be seen or to show who else has been sent the email
- when information is being sent to a group of customers but each customer's address needs to be kept private
- to keep an audit trail of emails.

Attachments

Revised

Attachments: are files sent with an email.

- They can increase the size of an email making it slow to send.
- Some attachments can contain a virus and so all emails should be virus scanned before they are opened.
- Attachments can be blocked or returned if the receiving email system considers them to be dangerous.
- Some attachments may be unreadable for the receiver as the correct software may not be installed on the receiving device.

Address books and contacts

Revised

Address book(s) are where all email addresses and other contact details, e.g. mobile phone numbers, are stored. Each entry is called a contact and can be edited if details change. Different lists can be set up within an address book, such as customers, employees or friends.

> **Exam tip**
> You should know how email can be used appropriately by businesses.

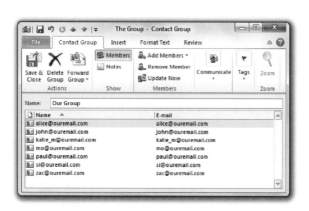 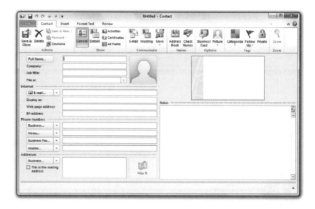

Email etiquette

There are some rules (netiquette) which should always be followed when using email. Some of these are:

- use an appropriate subject line
- follow the agreed email policy within the business
- check the message content before hitting the send button
- include a signature on any business emails
- be polite
- write in normal English with abbreviations used carefully
- do not write in capital letters
- check if the email should be replied to all the sending list or just the person the email was originally from
- when sending an attachment with an email, mention in the email body that there are file(s) attached.
- tell people the format of any attachments you send if they're anything other than standard, e.g. Microsoft Office file types

Check your understanding

8 Explain why a business may want to set up a distribution list for customers.

9 Identify two situations when the bcc facility could be used.

10 Describe two disadvantages relating to attachments.

11 Identify two email rules which relate to sending attachments.

Go online for answers

Diary management software (DMS)

Diary management software (DMS) enables employees, whatever their location, to co-ordinate their diaries but also to keep some things private.

DMS lets employees:

- check that everyone who is needed can attend an appointment/meeting
- make sure that appointments/meetings do not clash
- set reminders to make sure that meetings/appointments are not missed
- plan and track the progress of team projects
- allocate tasks to different members of the team
- communicate with each other to make sure that all tasks are completed
- share files and documents which are needed during the project.

A DMS can do the following.

- Create appointments/meetings – a DMS can create and store a list of appointments and who will be attending. Clashes between appointments/meetings will be shown and alternative times can be suggested.
- Invite participants – when an appointment/meeting has been created, the DMS can invite, by email, the people who need to attend it.
- Create tasks/projects – a DMS can provide a task list including who is to complete it and the deadline. The priority can also be set. Task lists can be shared with access to the lists controlled.
- Create to-do lists – these are usually small tasks which need to be completed and could be used as reminders – an electronic post-it note!
- Set reminders – reminders can be set to automatically remind people of an appointment/meeting. These can be set to activate at different times prior to the appointment/meeting. Reminders can be attached to tasks, and the people who need to complete the tasks.

Exam tip

You should be able to describe the tasks which can be completed using a DMS and be able to apply these to a given scenario.

How is a DMS accessed?

Revised

Many DMS systems are now cloud software applications – accessed through a web browser or mobile application.

A **mobile application (mobile app)** is a software application which is usually designed to run on smartphones.

The DMS would be stored and accessed through servers at a remote location to the business – the **cloud**. Changes made to the DMS and files which need to be accessed by users are also stored on these servers.

Employees who work remotely could access and use the DMS and any files/documents they need through a mobile app and the cloud environment.

A DMS can be closed or open.

● A **closed** DMS means that it is possible for just those people who have the access logins and passwords to have access.

● An **open** DMS means it can be accessed by anyone who is given the web address.

The **access rights** to the DMS are granted whether the access is:

● closed – people would be able to view, add or amend the facilities of the DMS

● open – people are only allowed to view the DMS.

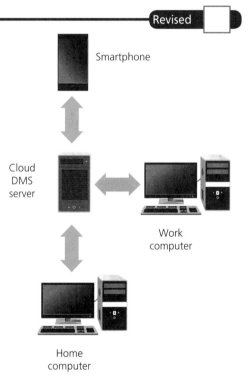

Exam tip

Make sure you understand how a DMS can be accessed by users and the different rights which can be granted.

Check your understanding

Tested

12 Identify three tasks which can be completed using a DMS.

13 Describe two advantages to employees of having a DMS stored on a cloud environment.

14 Describe what is meant by a closed DMS.

15 Identify and describe the different access rights which can be granted to the users of a DMS.

Go online for answers

Online

Creating and editing documents collaboratively

Document types

All businesses create documents including:

- invoices
- letters
- leaflets/brochures
- memos
- order forms
- presentations
- reports
- websites.

Documents can be:

- internal – can usually be seen only by those employees who work for the business
- external – can usually be seen by employees, customers of the business and the general public
- formal – such as a letter – have a formal layout/structure and use formal language and words
- informal – has a less structured layout/structure and will use a less formal style of writing.

Documents in shared access areas

Business documents can be created by a group/team of employees who may not be in the same location so all these employees will need to have access. This access can be:

- in shared areas on the business computer network. Different access levels can be set, e.g. write, edit and/or read.
- on a cloud so all team members can access documents online. The access levels can be set to open or restricted.

Inserting comments into an existing draft document

Revised ☐

This can be useful when editing/reviewing a document. Comments about a draft document can be inserted without having to produce a paper copy and write down the comments. The initials of the reviewer making the comments can be seen in the comment box.

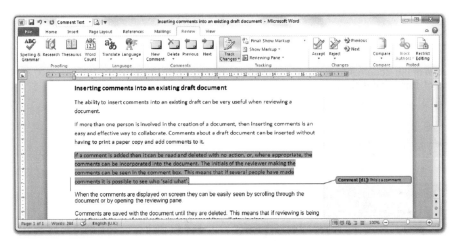

The comments can be seen by scrolling through the document, or by opening the reviewing pane. They are saved with the document until they are deleted.

Editing and track changes

Revised ☐

Documents can be reviewed and edited using the track changes facility with any changes made being seen in a different colour to the original text.

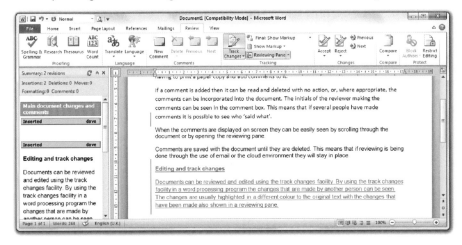

The word processing program will insert marks and details that show where deletions, insertions and formatting changes have been made. This is known as the **markup** version of the document.

The track changes facility allows many people to review and make changes to a document. In the situation below the comments/changes can be seen all together, separated by reviewer name.

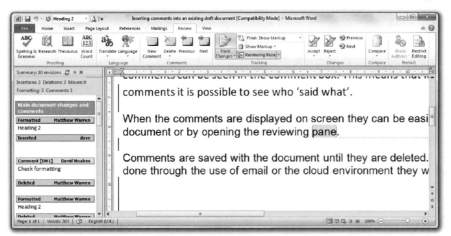

Reviewing facilities, accepting or rejecting changes made

Revised

The suggested changes can be accepted or rejected by the creator of the document.

In a team situation one person should be in charge of making changes to the document based on the comments and changes suggested by the rest of the team.

The other people involved in creating the document should be able to see and check any revisions made.

Changes can be dealt with one at a time or all at once. Comments can be read, actioned if appropriate and then deleted. Accepted changes become part of the final document.

> **Exam tip**
>
> You should be able to explain how documents can be created and edited collaboratively.
>
> You should be able to apply your knowledge of the appropriate use of the editing tools to a given scenario.

Check your understanding

Tested

16 Describe what is meant by a formal document.

17 Describe a shared access area.

18 Describe how comments can be used when a document is being reviewed by a team of people.

19 What is the markup version of a document?

Go online for answers

Online

Computer legislation and the CMA

What is computer legislation?

Revised

Laws have been passed in the UK, and elsewhere, to make illegal the misuse of computers to do harm to others, steal their ideas or their data or reveal information about others.

The laws do not stop people misusing computers, but they can act as a deterrent to try and prevent computer misuse and give victims of computer crime ways of recovering losses they may have suffered.

There are four main areas of laws which relate to the use of computers in the United Kingdom. These are:

- computer misuse
- health and safety
- data protection
- copyright.

> **Exam tip**
>
> Make sure that you understand and can explain how business users are affected by the Computer Misuse Act (CMA).
>
> Learn the three parts to the CMA and make sure that you will be able to apply these to a given scenario.
>
> Keep up to date with any changes to the CMA and how these will affect business users.

Computer Misuse Act (CMA)

Revised

This deals with problems relating to hacking and viruses.

The three main parts to this Act are:

1 Unauthorised access to computer material

   This relates to hacking – accessing data or programs that you do not have permission to view. Hacking is only illegal if you do not have permission to access the data or use the computer to access the data.

2 Unauthorised access with intent to commit or facilitate the commission of further offences

   If information is accessed, even with permission to do so, with the intention of using it to commit, e.g. fraud or blackmail, you are breaking this law.

3 Unauthorised acts with intent to impair or with recklessness as to impairing operation of a computer

   This means that any unauthorised alterations made to computer materials, e.g. changing files or data, is breaking this law. This includes sending a virus which makes a computer malfunction, alters how it works or damages other data.

Penalties for breaking this law can be a prison term of several years, or fines, or both.

The Computer Misuse Act 1990
- Unauthorised work
- Deliberate data destruction
- Fraud
- Program theft (software piracy)
- Data theft
- Planting of viruses
- Hacking

Check your understanding

Tested

1 Explain the term hacking.
2 Describe how the CMA could be used by a business if a virus was deliberately sent to their computer network.

Go online for answers

Online

Health and safety legislation

Health and safety at work

Health and safety in a workplace is the responsibility of everyone – employers, employees and visitors.

There are two parts to the legislation relating to health and safety. These are the responsibilities relating to the health and safety legislation (Health and Safety at Work Act) and the general health issues and physical safety of using computers in the workplace.

The main law covering the use of computer equipment is the Health and Safety (Display Screen Equipment) Regulations. To comply with these employers have to:

1   Analyse workstations and assess and reduce risks.
    The computer equipment and the area around it should be safe. If risks are identified then action must be taken to make the area safe.

2   Ensure that workstations meet the minimum requirements.
    Workstations should include tilt and swivel screens with enough space for a keyboard, monitor and paperwork. Adjustable chairs and suitable lighting should also be provided for employees.

3   Plan work so that there are breaks or changes of activity.
    Employees should not be expected to work at a computer all day. Regular breaks or a change in the activity that the employees are carrying out should be scheduled into the working day.

4   Arrange and pay for eye tests and glasses (if special ones are needed).
    Employees who work with computer equipment can have eye tests arranged and paid for. The eye test can be repeated at regular intervals. The employer will only have to pay for glasses if special ones are required.

5   Provide health and safety training and information.
    Training should be provided to make sure employees can use the computer equipment correctly. The training should include how to use the equipment to minimise risks to their health, and the steps that have been taken to minimise the risks.

Health issues

Issue	What this is	How it can be reduced
Repetitive Strain Injury (RSI)	• A range of conditions affecting joints and muscles in the neck, arms, shoulders wrists, hands and fingers. • Happens when the same muscles are used to perform the same actions repetitively, such as clicking mouse buttons or using a keyboard.	• Schedule regular breaks into the working day. • Provide ergonomically designed equipment including a keyboard, mouse and wrist rest for employees to use.
Headaches/Eye strain	• Blurred vision and a deterioration in eyesight. • Pain in the head, usually at the temples and above the eyes. • Happens when lighting is not suitable or through too much use of screens.	• Be provided with, and use, an anti-glare screen. • Use swivel bases on screens to deflect the light (natural and artificial). • Adjust brightness and contrast on screens. • Have regular eye checks – provided by employers.
Neck and back pain	• Discomfort and pain in the back and neck – can spread to the shoulders. • Happens when sitting in an incorrect posture.	• Schedule regular breaks into the working day. • Be provided with, and use, an adjustable chair with height and back adjustment. • Walk round to ease strain on muscles in back and shoulders.

Physical safety

A safe workplace is the responsibility of employers and employees. Employees should:

● use the ergonomic equipment, such as chairs, keyboards, mice and wrist rests, provided by their employers

● not drink or eat when using a computer due to the possible electrical hazards, and the possible spillage of food and drink into the computer itself

● not tamper with any cables or computer parts

● place the computer equipment safely so it cannot fall or be knocked over

● take care of their own health and safety and that of others.

> **Exam tip**
>
> Make sure you keep up to date with any changes in health and safety legislation and how these changes will affect employers and employees.
>
> You should be able to apply health and safety legislation to a given scenario.

Check your understanding

3 Describe two actions that an employer needs to carry out to comply with the Health and Safety Act.

4 Identify two health issues that can arise from working with computer equipment. For each give possible solutions.

Go online for answers

The Data Protection Act (DPA)

What is the DPA?

The DPA does not actually protect personal data but protects the rights of the owners of the data. It sets out rules (the 8 principles) on how the data should be stored and used by a business/organisation.

The DPA also provides a way for the owners of the data to complain and claim compensation if their personal data is misused.

Term	Explanation
Personal data	Any information about a living individual, facts (e.g. name, address and date of birth) and opinions, to allow the individual to be identified.
Data Subject	The person the data is being stored about.
Data User	The person who needs to access or use the data as part of their job.
Data Controller	This is the person who needs to apply for permission to collect and store data. They decide what data needs to be collected and what it will be used for and how.
Information Commissioner	This is the person who enforces the DPA and who organisations need to apply to in order to gain permission to collect and store personal data. They also make the general public aware of their rights under the DPA.

The 8 principles of the DPA

The 8 principles are that personal data must:

1 be fairly and lawfully processed

2 be processed for limited purposes

3 be adequate, relevant and not excessive

4 be accurate and up to date

5 not be kept for longer than is necessary

6 be processed in line with your rights

7 be kept secure

8 not be transferred to other countries outside of the European Economic Area that do not have adequate data protection.

Exam tip

Make sure you keep up to date with any changes in the DPA and how these will affect business users.

You should be able to apply the DPA to a given scenario and learn the actions a business needs to take to comply with the DPA.

Check your understanding

5 In a business, what is the difference between the data controller and a data subject?

6 How does the DPA try to protect individuals whose personal data is being stored by a business?

Go online for answers

The Copyright, Designs and Patents Act

Copyright

Revised

This act was first introduced in 1988 and makes it illegal to copy a work, e.g. a file, image or software, without permission from the owner or copyright holder. Owning the copyright to a piece of work will not stop others from copying it, but only allows the owner to bring action in the courts.

The main problem is that often the person copying the work cannot be traced, as copies of computer software, images and other digital data (such as audio and video files) are easily made and shared.

People and businesses who break this law risk having to pay a large fine.

The main ICT areas covered by this act are:

● software piracy – the illegal copying or downloading of software

● the use of ICT to copy or download files such as music, video or text, to avoid paying for these. This includes downloading files from the internet

● using software without the correct, or any, software licence

● theft by a business of the methods and ideas of other ICT businesses.

Software licensing

Revised

Software licensing is the main way in which this law is most commonly broken. If a piece of software has been bought by a business with a licence to install it on three PCs but it is installed on the network for all users to access, then they have broken this law.

If text, images and other files are **downloaded from the internet** and used then permission from the copyright holder must be obtained and acknowledged. A fee may need to be paid.

Any **copying or sharing of digital files**, e.g. mp3 files, DVDs, CDs and software, created by others is a breach of copyright and is illegal under the Copyright, Designs and Patents Act.

> **Exam tip**
>
> As with other acts and laws, you should be aware of any updates and how these will affect business users.
>
> You should be able to apply the Copyright, Designs and Patents Act to a given scenario.

Check your understanding

Tested

7 Describe how a business can comply with the Copyright, Designs and Patents Act when purchasing software.

8 State two actions that should be taken if a copyrighted image is to be used in a presentation.

Go online for answers

Online

Personal data and cyber bullying

As computer systems and the internet are used more, users need to be aware of actions which can have an impact on other users and businesses. Businesses and their employees need to consider the moral and ethical issues and the actions taken when using computer systems.

The use and abuse of personal and private data

Revised ☐

Every business holds personal and private data on its customers and employees. The data held will depend on the type of business.

The Data Protection Act (DPA) governs the use of this data and details the actions that can be taken by data subjects if their data is abused.

The Computer Misuse Act (CMA) makes it illegal to hack into a computer system and steal the data stored on it.

Errors and deliberate actions can happen when dealing with data.

● Changes/updates to data may not be saved. This means that one of the DPA principles – data must be accurate and up to date – has been broken.

● Files holding data may be overwritten, or deleted. This can be stopped by following a file naming policy.

● Data can be stolen which could lead to identity theft – taking over someone else's identity. Criminals could then use that identity to commit crimes.

● Employees could deliberately damage or destroy data files or give access details to someone else to enable then to get access to the data.

Legislation attempts to keep data from being abused. It does not stop people abusing data but, if caught, they can be punished.

Cyber bullying

Revised ☐

Cyber bullying is threatening or embarrassing someone using technology, e.g. a mobile phone or the internet. This means that embarrassing or horrid comments can be spread around the world in a matter of hours.

Cyber bullying can happen to anyone in school or in the workplace. It is important that a business recognises the importance of attempting to stop any employees carrying out cyber bullying and should have a section in its IT policy to cover this.

Check your understanding

Tested ☐

9 Describe an impact to customers of having their personal data stolen.

10 Explain how a file naming policy may reduce the risk of data being abused.

11 What is cyber bullying?

Go online for answers

Online ☐

Monitoring of individuals by organisations

Worker monitoring or logging Revised ☐

Businesses may need to monitor employees. Among the reasons for this are:

- business critical tasks are being completed
- an audit trail may be needed.

There are several ways in which employees and other individuals (e.g. customers) can be monitored.

Worker monitoring/logging can be done in many ways.

- **CCTV cameras** can monitor and record what employees are doing. Employees can view them as an invasion of privacy but a business can use them to protect its employees and the empty premises, e.g. at night or weekends.

- **Swipe** or **RFID ID** cards can be used to allow different access rights to each area of the premises. Their use will enable an audit trail to be created to show who went into each area of the premises and when.

Key logging Revised ☐

Key logging is hardware or software which records the real time activity of a computer user, including the keyboard keys they press, or collects screen captures (prints). If they are installed illegally they can be difficult to detect but anti-key logging software is available.

- An IT department can use them to troubleshoot technical problems with a computer system.

- A business can use them to create an audit trail of any websites visited or keys pressed by a computer user.

- Criminals use them on public computers to steal passwords or credit card information.

Normal key logging software stores data on the local/network hard drive, but some can automatically transmit data over the network to a remote computer or web server.

Mobile phone triangulation Revised ☐

Mobile phone triangulation is the obtaining of the current position of a mobile phone. This can help the emergency services to find the exact location that a call was made from. But this can invade the privacy of the phone user as it can allow someone to check where a person is without their consent.

Cookies

Revised

A **cookie** is a 'text file' which usually contains two pieces of information: a site name and unique user ID. They are downloaded the first time a website is accessed and can then be used to personalise the site the next time it is visited.

Cookies can:

- record how long is spent on each page of the website, what links are clicked and any accessibility options which are activated
- store data on what is in a 'shopping cart', adding items as the user clicks
- create a marketing list or target special offers which are relevant to the website users based on their previous browsing or shopping habits.

The use of cookies to collect and store personal information without permission is not strictly legal in the UK. Websites using cookies can state that by using that website a user is agreeing to download the cookies.

Most web browsers allow users to block cookies so a user can block all cookies or pick and choose which ones to accept.

Worker call monitoring or recording

Revised

Worker call monitoring/recording can have an impact on the workers. It can:

- help workers keep on track with the tasks they have to complete
- improve productivity
- enable employers to reward those employees who are most productive
- encourage some workers to work longer than they are contracted to do.

The recording and monitoring of calls can:

- enable an audit trail to be kept in case of any future issues or questions
- be used for training employees to deal with complicated calls from, for example, customers
- assist in employees keeping to the terms of a policy about taking or making private calls during working hours.

Electronic consumer surveillance

Revised

Electronic consumer surveillance usually involves a loyalty card scheme. This works by:

- allocating points to the card when a customer uses the business
- converting points into vouchers at regular intervals
- letting the customer spend, save or exchange the vouchers for goods or services.

The loyalty card lets a business keep track of every transaction made by a customer. They can use this information to target offers to specific customers. For example, customers who buy cat food will receive offers relating to cat merchandise.

The information gathered by loyalty cards can also be used by the businesses that are linked to the issuing business, called affiliates. These affiliates will also use the information to target specific marketing information to the customers.

Issues to be considered

Revised

There are many ways in which individuals can be monitored by organisations. Each will have impacts on the business, employees and customers. The impact and how this affects the group of people can be seen in different ways. For example, the impact a business sees as positive may be seen by employees as negative.

As the use of computers in a business setting increases it is important that the moral and ethical issues and the impact these have on the business, employees and customers is considered when storing personal and private data.

> **Exam tip**
>
> When revising this topic you should consider the moral and ethical issues, including the monitoring of individuals, which can affect business computer users.
>
> The issues should be considered from the point of view of the business, its employees and customers.

Check your understanding

Tested

12 Explain how swipe cards can be used to protect the premises of a business.

13 Describe how key logging could be used by criminals.

14 Describe one disadvantage of the use of mobile phone triangulation.

15 What is meant by a cookie?

16 Describe one advantage to a business of monitoring/recording calls.

17 Describe two impacts on employees of calls being monitored or recorded.

Go online for answers

Online

Data loss, corruption and theft

If data held on a business computer system is lost, corrupted or stolen there can be a serious impact on the running of the business and on its customers and employees.

Legal implications

Revised

There are two main Acts which relate to the loss and theft of data.

● Data Protection Act (DPA) – if business data is lost or stolen, e.g. by a hacker, the Information Commissioner can take action against the business as the DPA states that personal data must be kept secure. The business may have to pay financial compensation to any person whose data has been lost or stolen.

● Computer Misuse Act (CMA) – if data is stolen through hacking then, if the hacker is traced, the CMA enables them to be prosecuted. The hacker can be sent to prison and/or fined.

Impact on customers

Revised

If the personal data of customers is lost, stolen or corrupted then this can have a serious impact on them and the business.

Customers may:

● lose confidence and trust in the business and may move their custom (also an impact on the business)

● become victims of identity theft.

Impact on employees

Revised

If an employee loses, steals or corrupts data then this can have a huge impact on them, including breaking their IT policy. The IT policy sets down rules about data and the actions that could be taken if any of these rules are broken.

The actions an employee faces could be:

● a formal written warning

● a demotion in job role, and probably a reduction in salary

● dismissal from their job

● a reference which stated why they lost their job – this could result in difficulty in finding another job.

The employer could also increase security including:

● access rights to data being changed

● more monitoring of what employees are doing whilst accessing the data.

Impact on the business (organisation)

This can be very serious for the business.

Under the legislation relating to this a business will have to pay **compensation** to the owners of the data. The amount of compensation can be very high and can increase if more than one person is affected.

If the business cannot pay the compensation it may have to close as it does not have any money to either pay the compensation or to carry on trading.

The business will also have to increase the level of **security** – its systems and premises. This can be expensive in terms of purchase, installation and maintenance costs.

Their **customers** could lose confidence and take their custom elsewhere leading to financial problems – a business needs customers to carry on trading.

> **Exam tip**
>
> You need to know the implications and consequences of data loss, corruption and theft.
>
> These implications and consequences should be considered from the viewpoint of the customers, employees and the business.

Check your understanding

18 Describe two impacts on the employees of a business if they lose data.

19 Describe one impact on a customer of having their data stolen from a business computer system.

20 Describe two impacts on a business of having data stolen from their computer system.

21 Explain how the CMA can be used if data is stolen through hacking.

22 Describe the security costs to a business of having data stolen.

23 Explain how the DPA can be used if data is lost or stolen.

Go online for answers

Threats to data security

Different types of threats

As computer systems and the internet are used more in business so the threats have increased.

These can impact on the running of a business as computer systems and data need to be protected, including financial transactions carried out on the internet.

The most common threats are shown below.

> **Exam tip**
> You should be able to describe the most common threats to data security and explain the impact these threats may have on a business and its customers.

Threat	Description
Computer **virus**	A program that replicates and spreads attempting to make a system unreliable. It spreads by infecting files on a network system or a file system that is accessed by other computers.
Trojan	Appears to be something wanted or needed by the user but is a program designed to give full control of a PC to another. It can be hidden in valid programs and software. Trojan horses can make copies of themselves, steal information, or harm their host computer systems.
Worm	A standalone program that replicates to spread to other computers, e.g. through a network. Worms always cause harm to a network, e.g. by consuming bandwidth.
Phishing	A way of attempting to acquire private information, by pretending to be from a trustworthy source. Usually carried out by email spoofing or instant messaging with users asked to enter details on a fake website.
Spyware	Malicious software (malware) usually secretly installed on a system to collect information and data, e.g. user logins, financial information, without user's knowledge. Some spyware such as key loggers may be installed to intentionally monitor users. They can: • be hidden from the user and difficult to detect • install additional software or redirect web browsers to different websites • change computer settings which could lead to slow internet connection speeds or changes in web browser settings.
Physical threats (e.g. loss/theft of devices)	Computer system components – keyboards, monitors, memory sticks/removable storage devices, base units – can be easily lost or stolen. The most common of these are memory sticks and portable storage devices.
Adware (Advertising-supported software)	A program automatically showing adverts to generate revenue for the author. Usually harmless but can include spyware such as key loggers. Adware can be found in: • a pop up • the user interface of a software package • an installation screen.
Hacking	Finding the weaknesses of a system to exploit them. A hacker is someone who finds the weaknesses in a system to gain unauthorised access. A hacker may be motivated by a multitude of reasons, such as profit, protest, or challenge.
Denial of Service (DoS) attacks	An attempt to make a computer or network system unavailable to its users. A DoS is usually focused on preventing an internet site or service from functioning efficiently or at all, temporarily or indefinitely. DoS attacks usually target sites/services hosted on high-profile web servers, e.g. banks, payment websites (e.g. PayPal).

24 Describe how a computer virus can spread.

25 Describe the difference between adware and spyware.

26 Identify where adware could be found.

27 Give one situation when spyware can be deliberately installed.

28 Define the term 'hacker'.

29 Describe how a DoS attack can affect an internet site.

Go online for answers | Online

Actions to minimise risks

Actions can be taken to reduce the risks and threats of using computer systems. Some of these actions can be taken by the users of the computer systems and others can be provided by software.

Online protection

The internet is a great place to spend time but there are also criminals looking to hijack your computer and steal your identity and money.

Online criminals can:

● infect a computer system with spyware, pop ups and viruses to steal personal details and identities

● take over a computer system and use it to attack other computer systems

● send spam and scam emails

● create fake websites

● hack into a network

● use email and chat to bully, con or cheat.

Protection on the internet can be achieved by users considering the following points:

Sharing information

People using social networking and blog sites need to be careful about the personal information, e.g. date of birth, address, they put on these sites.

The information can be deleted but there is no control over how it is stored, copied or archived. Identity thieves can piece together a person's identity from a variety of sources to get all the details they need.

Use different passwords for different sites

It can be difficult to remember lots of different passwords but the same password should not be used for multiple websites. By using different passwords, if the password for your social network site was stolen then this would not expose the password for your online banking account.

Always check a website for the padlock symbol

If sensitive personal data (address details, phone numbers, bank details, etc.) needs to be inputted into a website then the padlock symbol should be displayed. This means that the data will be encrypted during transmission over the internet.

Beware of unsolicited/unknown senders of emails

Don't open emails where the sender's address is unknown as these can contain links to code that can infect a computer. If the email is opened then any links in the email body should not be followed and the email should not be replied to.

Protection software and hardware

Software and hardware can be used to protect and increase the security of data and systems. As long as these are used and kept up to date they can offer some protection to threats to data security.

Firewalls

A **firewall** controls what data can and cannot pass through it.

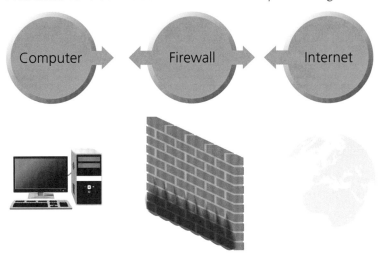

A firewall can be software or hardware.

● Software: many operating systems include software-based firewalls to protect against threats from the internet. Free firewall packages can be downloaded from the internet. A business may decide to buy a software firewall which can include anti-virus and anti-spam software.

● Hardware: these are much faster than software firewalls but are more expensive and tricky to set up.

The type and number of firewalls used will depend on the sensitivity of the data being held. The more valuable or sensitive the data is then the higher the level of protection expected by the business and the people whose data is being held.

Anti-virus software

Anti-virus software detects a virus before it enters the computer system. If a virus is detected then the software will automatically quarantine it or ask the user what action should be taken.

Anti-virus software must be kept up to date. When it is bought and installed it is the most up-to-date version. As new viruses are created and distributed all the time, patches will be released to reduce the risk of the new viruses.

Automatically scheduled anti-virus scans can be carried out to search for viruses on the computer which have not been detected by the anti-virus software.

Anti-spam software

Anti-spam software can be part of an anti-virus software package. It can be set up to run automatically or on user defined options set during installation.

Spam is the sending of unwanted messages, often unsolicited advertising, to a large number of email addresses. Spam can be a security concern as it can deliver Trojan horses, viruses, worms, spyware, and targeted phishing attacks.

Data encryption software

Data encryption software encrypts data so that only users with the unlock code/secret key can read/use the data which has been transmitted.

For example, a user needs to encrypt and send the phrase

The cat sat on the mat

This phrase would be received by the receiving computer system as

51gP!6n!6K*61gB!6

Phrases can only be unencrypted if the receiving system has the secret key which has to be kept secure and only accessed by trustworthy people.

Data can be stored/saved in an encrypted form. The secret key will be needed to unlock the data if it is to be used.

Check your understanding
Tested

30 Identify three activities carried out by online criminals.

31 What does the padlock symbol on a website denote?

32 Why should care be taken when receiving unsolicited emails?

33 What is the purpose of a firewall?

34 What is spam?

35 Explain how data encryption can be used to keep data secure.

Go online for answers
Online

Automatic and manual updating facilities for operating systems and security software

Automatic updates

Most software vendors will make changes and updates to their software after release – these are **patches**. Patches attempt to resolve any identified potential security issues.

The updating of operating systems and security software can be done automatically or manually.

Automatic updates for operating system software usually happen when the computer system is going through the shutdown process.

The vendor will specify a point in the shutdown process where the operating system will download updates released since the last shutdown process was carried out.

At the end of the updating procedure the computer system will automatically shut down without any intervention from the user.

Automatic updates for security (anti-virus) software are done in real time – when the computer system is connected to the internet the security software is constantly checking for new updates which are automatically installed.

The advantage of automatic updates is that the user does not have to remember to update. This will be automatically carried out keeping the computer system as secure as possible.

Manual updates

Manual updates for software can be completed on an ad-hoc basis or can be set to be checked at a specified time by a user. Users can look at the updates to decide whether or not to download them.

Disadvantages include:

● they can be forgotten, leaving the computer system vulnerable to threats

● the time it can take to download the patch

● there may be a time delay between the patch being released and the manual update

● the computer system must be switched on and connected to the internet for the update to be downloaded.

Check your understanding

36 State one advantage to the user of using the automatic update facility.

37 Identify two disadvantages of manually updating software.

Go online for answers